KU-784-725

HANDMADE

SIRI HELLE

HANDMADE

Learning the Art of Chainsaw
Mindfulness in a Norwegian Wood

Translated from the Norwegian by
Kari Dickson and Lucy Moffatt

GRANTA

Granta Publications, 12 Addison Avenue, London W11 4QR

First published in Great Britain by Granta Books, 2022

Copyright © Siri Helle, 2020
Translation © Kari Dickson and Lucy Moffatt, 2022

First published in Norwegian as *Med Berre Nevane* by Samlaget, 2020.
Published in agreement with Northern Stories.

Siri Helle has asserted her moral right under the
Copyright, Designs and Patents Act, 1988, to be identified as the
author of this work. Kari Dickson and Lucy Moffatt have asserted their
moral rights under the Copyright, Designs and Patents Act, 1988,
to be identified as the translators of this work.

All rights reserved. This book is copyright material and must not
be copied, reproduced, transferred, distributed, leased, licensed or
publicly performed or used in any way except as specifically permitted
in writing by the publisher, as allowed under the terms and conditions
under which it was purchased or as strictly permitted by applicable
copyright law. Any unauthorized distribution or use of this text may
be a direct infringement of the author's, translators' and publisher's
rights, and those responsible may be liable in law accordingly.

This translation has been published with
the financial support of NORLA.

A CIP catalogue record for this book is available
from the British Library.

1 3 5 7 9 10 8 6 4 2

ISBN 978 1 78378 747 0
eISBN 978 1 78378 748 7

Typeset in Galliard by Patty Rennie
Printed and bound by CPI Group (UK) Ltd, Croydon, CR0 4YY

www.granta.com

To the wisest hands I know.
Thank you for your help, patience and love.

CONTENTS

INTRODUCTION

*In which my hands teach me a
new way of looking at the world*

It's far too warm out in the baking sun. Far too warm for protective clothing, ear defenders and a hot chainsaw; too warm for the chopping block and axe. The sweat streams off me, mingling with the sawdust and needles from the spruce tree I'm working on. I drink and drink from the river that runs past the cabin, but never quench my thirst. And still I press on.

It isn't because I must. No one is paying me to chop down this tree, strip its branches, cut it into suitably sized chunks, split them into logs and stack them along the back wall of my small cabin. No one would blame me if I decided to stop and opted instead to lie on a rock in the river dangling my feet in the water, say – or do what I actually ought to be doing: working at home on my computer.

And yet, there's one thing I know for sure:

there's nothing I'd rather be doing. Once I get into the flow of log-splitting, once I find my rhythm with the logs and axe, I can keep going for any amount of time. The work fills my body, the repetition fills my head and, right now, this – chopping my own firewood – is the meaning of life itself.

And my thoughts run free. It was probably one time when I was standing there chopping, cutting and splitting, that it dawned on me: my hands are how I make sense of the world.

My hands – what they can and can't do – are what give me joy and a sense of achievement. I can sum up most of what is right and wrong with society in terms of my hands.

This is the story of how I found my way back to my own hands and to feeling at home in a cabin. It is the story of how I followed the urge to create and a vague desire to build something by hand – combined with a considerable fear of failing. And about how that desire ended up becoming a reality – in the form of an outside toilet.

*

I love building things. Making things. Producing, creating, bringing things about. And I hate making things. Both statements are equally true. What makes the difference? To some extent the tools, but most of all the sense of mastery. It doesn't necessarily matter to me whether I succeed at the first attempt; what matters is whether I feel I have some chance of succeeding eventually.

And those two things – the fact that I like to make stuff and that I have to work to achieve it – are precisely what I wish somebody had told me earlier. As a girl who was good at school, the obvious choice was to take subjects that would open the door to university. And then go there to study.

But that isn't what happened. I tried university, but found it incredibly slow and boring: and I certainly couldn't find the patience to wait five years for a master's degree before being allowed my own opinion. Instead I committed myself to political work within environmental organisations and squatting movements; I worked in kindergartens and healthcare and I hitchhiked back and forth across Europe a few times, never planning more than six months ahead – until, when I was twenty-nine, I started a practical course in agri-culture. And there, among milking cups that got stuck in the wrong places, goats that dissed me, potatoes that got impaled on my fork and an axe that wouldn't land where I wanted it to, I discov-ered what I'd been missing all those years. I hadn't been using my whole self. I had forgotten my body. Forgotten my hands.

I don't think I'm alone in this, so this book isn't just about me. Workers – craftspeople – are neces-sary and we must fight with all our might to retain them. But if we are to truly see and value their work, they can't be the only people with practical knowledge of it.

We can't all be craftspeople; we can't all have practical jobs. We can't all whittle our own cutlery, produce our own food or build our own privies. But having had this experience of making some-thing by hand, I believe that everybody should at least have a chance to use their whole self in this way.

What happens to the body when it's no longer used regularly for physical labour? What happens to our hands? And what happens to the society we have spent time and effort creating?

Once upon a time, most of us were ropemakers. Back then, we stripped the bark from lime trees in the spring, left it to soak over the summer and made lime bast rope out of the sodden fibres. We knew every millimetre of the finished product and knew what it was good for, and how much work went into it. As a result we took care of it, and we would even trust our children's lives to it, because we could trust what we knew. Nowadays, we can't do that anymore – and have to rely on CE safety labels instead.

If we can no longer replace a zip, we become reliant on cheap shop-bought trousers. The fewer tyres we change, the less we know about the car we entrust our lives to. The fewer people there are who know how much work goes into refitting a window or growing a cauliflower, the more difficult it is for carpenters and farmers to get fairly paid. I could go on and on.

Over the past century or so, the majority of us have gone from being producers to consumers, from creators to thinkers, from practitioners to theorists. This transition is one of the greatest changes in our modern society. And yet we hardly talk about it.

We modern Westerners are trained to do specialised salaried work and, other than that, we buy whatever we need to live. Not only were we not designed for this kind of existence – most of us don't even want to live this way.

But are we in any way encouraged to develop our useful, practical, wise hands? No. We advise bright young people to choose a life behind an office desk, and only those who don't thrive within an academic environment are expected to learn a practical trade.

Yet nobody is born to a manual trade or craft. Everybody has to start somewhere. And having the opportunity to learn – to go from bad to better and, eventually, good enough; becoming proficient in a skill – is a truly remarkable experience.

Getting the axe to hit the log just where I want it to, not once but every time, gave me a sense of achievement that little else can measure up to. And I think that learning to use an axe should be as natural a part of building a fully rounded person (which is what growing up is about) as learning about Ibsen.

This instinctive feeling of satisfaction tells us something about a need that life in the knowledge society can't satisfy. It's what makes us buy books about firewood, campfires and barns, and take up beer brewing and knitting. We all have within us the creative urge: the urge to perform a task that produces an outcome without the need for external recognition.

In many ways, this book is a paradox. I, the writer, will go on to claim that we should all have a chance to use our hands for practical purposes, and increase our appreciation of craftwork and the manual trades; yet I earn my own living at a computer, thinking and typing. When I was thirty, I got my first column – 'From the serving dish' in *Dag og Tid* newspaper. I had plenty to say and a way of conveying it. It was fairly easy to get people to listen to the thoughts, experiences and knowledge I gradually acquired about food, food production and the primary industries. Suddenly I was 'something in the media'. It was what everyone wanted to be ten years ago. And that's what

I still am. I get paid to write and have opinions about various things.

Of course I like writing. I like the feeling of being able to describe something precisely, something really complex and important. I like being able to communicate feelings to others in a way that enables them to understand too, maybe even share in my experiences, thoughts and opinions. I like the feeling of my fingers flying across the keyboard, almost faster than thought at times. I like words and I like having the opportunity to engage in public debate. But my job isn't the most important thing I do. Nor does it let me use my whole self.

But building a privy, a privy that is the only one of its kind in the entire world, did force me to use my whole self. And if it's possible to get such a sense of achievement, of experience, of identity and roots – not to mention sheer fun – from building such a tiny, simple building, how much more creative joy might there be out in the world just waiting for someone to tap into it?

We cannot go back in time. We cannot, should not and do not all wish to become self-sufficient. But equally, we cannot, should not and must not lose all contact with our working hands.

ONE

In which I learn to love a chainsaw

The tree doesn't want to fall. I'm alone at the cabin, trying to clear some trees from the land that runs down towards the river, and the big spruce closest to the cabin wall doesn't want to come down. I tug with all my might, drive in all the wedges I have to hand, but the tree stands just as firm. Worse still, I was so eager to make sure I sawed the entire trunk that I cut through the hinge I'd left between the felling cut and the directional notch. There is now a large hole in the hinge along which the tree is supposed to snap neatly, if it's to fall in the direction I want it to. The hole is in the middle, thankfully, but all the same: the tree is still standing and I don't know how much it is standing on. Damn.

I knew the tree would be difficult, that it wouldn't fall by itself. It had too many branches on the wrong side for that to happen. The Sitka spruces my paternal grandfather diligently planted in the post-war years are now so densely packed together that they let in no sunlight and there's no more room for branches in the middle of the cluster of trees, so they have to grow outwards, towards the walls of my cabin. I can't fell the tree in that direction.

That's why I've been putting this off. I stand beneath the tree, arms around its trunk as I peer up to calculate its centre of gravity. I agree with myself that it could be worse, but it could certainly be better too. And there's no denying the trunk is the broadest I've dealt with up here. It's around half a metre in diameter, just shy of the girth that would give me the excuse that the chainsaw blade is too short. Felling this tree shouldn't be a problem. As long as I don't do anything wrong.

I have what many Norwegians would still call a real cabin. It is located about half an hour's walk from Holmedal, the small village beside Dalsfjord where I grew up, out towards the coast in pretty much the heart of Sogn og Fjordane county. There's no access by road and the cabin is around

25 square metres, with no electricity or running water. In the early 1950s when my grandfather, Steinar Helle, had the cabin moved up here – into the mountains behind Holmedal – it really was on the mountainside too, open and with a view.

That's no longer the case. He planted so many trees that it's now more like the little house in the big woods.

But it's so lovely. The two-kilometre walk from the road with a height gain of 300 metres is just far enough to get your heart rate up and your mental pulse down, but not so far that you can't carry most things up. Once there, the cabin is in a beautiful spot beside a river that is always deep enough to swim in, often just too deep to ford and full of the freshest water imaginable. The cabin has a cast-iron wood-burner that is used both for cooking and heating the cabin, a fireplace, the world's tiniest kitchen, home-made cabin furniture, and far too many old paraffin lamps that I can't bring myself either to throw out or use.

I inherited the cabin after my father died. It took me many years to realise just what a treasure it was, but over the past six or seven years, this is where I've felt most at home. Maybe it's all about having a project: my grandfather planted the trees, but he would agree with me that they have now outlived their usefulness. It is time to clear them away, to recover the view and the sunlight.

My cabin is also a small part of my family's tiny chapter of industrial history. My grandfather didn't build the cabin himself. It was built as part of a student project at the carpentry school that was based in Holmedal in those days.

The finished cabin was supposed to be raffled off in the village. My grandfather didn't win, but he did pull rank. He was the factory director and if the factory director wanted to have the cabin, he got it.

It was, in fact, far from inevitable that my grandfather would become a factory director. He had originally emigrated to America, intending to build a life there. One of the coolest things I could show to my friends as a kid was the now-sealed pistol he'd carried when he worked as a longshoreman on the Chicago docks in the days of Al Capone.

While my grandfather was in America, my grandmother was still at home, working as a teacher in Holmedal. The plan was for her to emigrate too. According to family lore, her ticket was bought and her suitcase packed when the letter arrived: America had been rocked by a crisis – the Great Crash, of course. Steinar had lost his job, so she must not leave; he would come home instead. That letter feels like the most important one in my life, because if it had arrived just days later, my grandmother would already have left and they would probably have ended up staying, despite the crisis, and I would never have been born. But that's another story.

So my grandfather came home. With empty pockets and no job to go to. His brother Sigmund, who ran the family farm in Holmedal, was struggling too. The farm didn't yield a living, but there was a forge and their father, who had been the village blacksmith, had taught them to use it.

So they started to do just that. To forge. They made knife blades, with handles and sheaths, and they sold them – locally at first. Then larger markets opened up, so my grandfather crammed his saddlebags with knives, got on his bike and pedalled off, over the mountains and all the way to the capital, Oslo. There he sold knives for 40 øre apiece. And they sold well. By the time he cycled back home, his wallet was bulging, so much so that he treated himself to an overnight stay at a guest house at the top of the mountain. He put his wallet under his pillow, where it was sure to be safe.

Next morning he got up, climbed on his bike and freewheeled down the mountain. At the foot, he decided to buy a cup of coffee and reached for his wallet – which wasn't there. It was still lying where he'd left it: under the pillow at the top of the mountain. There was nothing for it but to pedal back up and fetch it.

He finally arrived home with his wallet, and an order for 200 knives. The celebrations must have raised the roof. It's a story I still love to this day.

My grandmother and grandfather both died before I was born, so I never got to meet them, but through stories like this, they were – are – still close by. The factory Steinar founded was part of my childhood too. By the time I was born, it had long since moved out of the tiny farm forge and into a former butter factory in Holmedal, but it continued to produce the famous Helle knives. At peak staff levels, the factory employed more than 100 people.

When my father, Svein, succeeded his father to become the factory director, I'd often go there after school. First, I'd visit my father's office. Sometimes there'd be a square of chocolate to be had from a cigar box. But the most exciting thing was being allowed to walk through the heavy doors, down into the factory itself.

Inside, the place was glowing red and hot yet tidy, I recall; all sparks and dust and smells. Mostly the smell of steel – still the scent of childhood for me – but also wood where they were working on handles. Hides and leather in the sheath department. Linseed oil. Tobacco. Instant coffee. In my memory, the men who worked there all wore checked shirts, leather aprons and had leathery skin on the palms of their hands, hands that could touch almost any part of those knife blades that ended up so sharp, without doing themselves an injury.

Yet the clearest thing of all was the noise: 'Ker-thud, ker-thud-thud.'

The drop-hammer stood alone in a corner, but for me it was the beating heart of the factory.

'Ker-thud, ker-thud-thud,' it went, again and again and again: 'Ker-thud, ker-thud-thud,' as it slammed down on the steel, and out of the steel came knife blades, square and useless for now, but the process was underway.

I was born in 1982. In my lifetime alone, a lot has changed in Norway. Factory sounds have vanished. Thirty per cent of the jobs in Norway's mainland industrial sector (excluding oil) have gone. As a share of total employment, industrial jobs in Norway have halved. The other practical professions have suffered the same fate: there are now only a third as many farmers and around half as many miners.

The simple fact is that the majority of Norwegians no longer work in farming and fishing. We no longer work in dairies, fish-landing stations, abattoirs or canning factories either. The number of people employed in factories of any kind is steadily dwindling.

Most of us now work in the next link in the chain. Job numbers in the tertiary sector – sales and servicing, communication and information, consultancy and services – are rising steadily.

But there's been an even more dramatic increase elsewhere: in my lifetime, the number of jobs in information and communication has almost doubled, and it has more than doubled in public administration.[1]

Today, most working Norwegians are employed to monitor, correct, plan and describe – and we largely leave the execution part to other people.

But of course, there are exceptions to this general shift away from practical work. Some 4,500 Norwegians still work in the textile, clothing and leatherware industries, and the number of jobs in building and construction has almost doubled since I was born.[2] Every single day, every single morning, before you're even out of bed, you benefit greatly from the fact that some people still work with their hands. We are utterly reliant on those who have practical jobs, who build and make physical things that must be robust and last, or be used until they are worn out or consumed or get recycled.

Regardless of how post-industrial we like to consider ourselves as a society, nearly all the physical things around us have one common feature:

somebody has made them. Even if that someone has increasingly been aided by one or more machines, this last point is unavoidable: the only thing we still can't eliminate from the 'production' equation is the human being.

Warm feelings for cold steel

It's been far too many years since I was last here, but here I am: home in Holmedal, back at the knife factory down on the docks. The moment I open the door, I'm in the grip of time. The sensation of this door, which is heavy but glides smoothly on its hinges, the smell, the brick walls, the steps I'd recognise anywhere.

I have feelings for this factory. When I walk into this place, there is no way I can be anything other than 100 per cent subjective. While that may not usually be a goal for journalists and writers, I take pride in it right now. Because I'm far from alone in having feelings for something as cold and hard as steel.

My second cousin, Jan Steffen Helle, has them too.

'It's always been industry for me. And always steel.'

Although he is part of a new generation, in a sense he has gone back to an old art. My father was the factory director, but not a smith. He was a business economist with a passion for the craft, the know-how and the product – but when it came to making the knives, he couldn't do it. Nor can my brother, Svein-Erik, who recently took the helm as director.

But Jan Steffen Helle? He can do it, and now he is head of production. His journey back to Holmedal and the knife factory started at secondary school, when a tour of a nearby technical college set him on the path to training as a plate welder.

'I had above-average marks at secondary school, so all hell broke loose at home, but I instantly felt I'd found something that would suit me,' Jan Steffen tells me.

It turned out to be the perfect choice. First, he got a certificate of apprenticeship, then he did a welding course at a technical college, and after that he settled in Bergen, with a job in the oil industry. Eventually he moved back home and started on the production side at the knife factory, initially working just a few hours a week. By now he has experience of working at most of the stations on the production line and is ready to take responsibility for the whole process.

A Helle knife is a functional knife with a blade made from three layers of laminated steel, a handle made of wood or a combination of wood, leather and bone, and a leather sheath. Between thirty and forty different models with different applications are in production at any given time, including jack knives, scouting knives for children, fish knives, whittling knives and hunting knives.

The factory staff use three different skills to produce each sports knife they make. There's steelwork – the blade is stamped, tempered, sharpened and polished. Then woodwork – the handle is dried, milled, oiled and polished in the factory. Finally, leatherwork is needed for the sheath and it is all done on-site – the leather is sewn, pressed and dried in-house.

There are many reasons to feel proud. Proud of being an industry based on craft; even though the knife blades have long been forged by machine, the final polish and the finishing touches to both blades and handles are still done by hand. Proud of having survived eighty-six years in business, and of the fact that this is the sole remaining factory in the village (where once there were many), and the only knife manufacturer in Norway that covers every step of the process.

In some ways, the factory feels like a museum – because much of its machinery is fifty years old and/or built on-site. Here, a really good employee needs to be an Inspector Gadget type because, far from being a museum, this is a productive and profitable factory.

Although staff numbers have fallen from more than 100 in my grandfather's day to 19 today, production has remained pretty constant. Of course, that means more machines – the first robots were introduced as early as 1989 and more have followed – but humans are still very much part of the equation.

I'm not alone in thinking there's something special about the sound of the drop-hammer at work, it isn't just my nostalgia – Jan Steffen feels the same, even though for him, it's his everyday life, future, income, responsibility.

'I didn't start working here because I felt I had to,' Jan Steffen says. 'It is partly the family history, but there is something else. I can't explain it. It's just a drive, I suppose.'

Why say 'just' when the drive is everything? If we look at the statistics, we find that the more engaged we are in our jobs, the better we perform. Still, I don't need any statistics. I can look around me right here – whether in the handle department, where the handles are tumbled in linseed oil, first in an old cement mixer and then in oak barrels; or up in the office, where there are knives everywhere and there's still only instant coffee to be had, just like when my father worked here – and feel that if there's no room for this kind of craft in Norway today, then Norway is the one with a problem, not the factory. Of course, I am part of this family of knife makers and I see the shadow of my father everywhere, but even so I am not the only one who thinks there is something of value here. Young people travel from far and wide to buy Helle knives from the place where they're made. The Instagram account of this tiny, ageing factory has more than 26,000 hip young followers – and there's no harm in a spot of industrial romanticism: it's what gives us our roots. Steel gives us roots because it's alive and has its place and takes up space. And now I'll go back to my mountain cabin in the woods with my knife in my belt, because that's where I need it, and I'll take extra special care of it, because it means something to me.

Every time I use it, I think about that, and I feel lucky to have this connection with the tool in my hand.

Small woman versus big tree

I first learned to use a chainsaw at agricultural college in Aurland, when I was twenty-nine years old.

I can still say with absolute certainty that I learned more in the two years I studied there than I've learned in the rest of the thirty-five years I have lived put together. Yet the very first thing I discovered was quite the opposite: how little I knew.

I soon found out that the milking shed was where I wanted to be. I fell in love with the inquisitive goat noses that nuzzled at my face. With the long cow tongues that rasped up my back as I walked past the feeder with a bucket of cattle feed. Even on the coldest, darkest winter mornings, my hands warmed up quickly when they were placed around a soft, milk-filled udder. The day brightened up the instant a nimble kid playfully bounded sideways along the floor of the milking shed, all four legs off the ground.

I settled into the routines and repetition. At first I was clumsy and hesitant, but if you do something often enough, you quickly improve. I started to realise that most things must – and can – be learned, from how much hay to load on the fork for every heave, to how to attach the cups directly onto the cow's teats without any of the clumsy fiddling that lets air and possibly harmful bacteria into the milking system. It seemed impossible at first, but every day it got a bit easier and my sense of achievement made me strong – inside and out.

I had always craved that sense of mastery. I had just never realised it until then, because I've always been so restless.

I remember at primary school having to run around all the buildings at break-time to work off the tingling feeling I got in my body after sitting still for a whole lesson. I forced myself to do it because I wanted to be as good as I was expected to be. Before I was even five, my mother noticed I would correct her when she read aloud to me – because I could read for myself. I even remember the first thing I read: a story in the comic book about 'Teddy the World's Strongest Bear' where his arch-enemy, Croesus Vole, is a pirate. The comic was lying on the living room table, which was at perfect standing height for me.

I realised I had a sharp mind and that it was meant to be used – my eagerness to learn was well above average when I started school and I generally ploughed through the exercises in my Norwegian textbooks a lot faster than the teachers might have wished. Keeping me happy was probably a challenge: I got bored quickly.

I took some of my boredom out on these same teachers. It was easy to find out who I could get away with bothering, including the teacher who didn't have the nerve to get angry when he had his bottom poked with a pair of compasses. Some of it I took out on my fellow pupils. At primary school I had fights that were more than playful with all three boys in my class and the one in the year above.

The rest of it I ran, played and climbed off. For as long as I was allowed to be childishly fond of climbing, and a good while after, it was a favourite pastime – clambering up trees and crags and cliffs. There were two enormous copper beeches opposite the house where I grew up, and I'd shin up them wearing a bicycle helmet when Mum was watching. Everywhere else, I'd climb at least as high bareheaded. The meadow below the house was becoming overgrown with branchy willow trees and that was all the gym equipment I needed. The spruce trees at the far end of the meadow behind the house were dense with branches and I could easily climb a long way up. The crags down towards the fjord were steep and exciting.

Although all this scrabbling about and scaling trees and rocks didn't earn me nearly as much praise as my Norwegian essays or the many English verbs I eventually memorised, it was probably just as important for my sense of self – and just as essential for my good results at school.

*

At secondary school, my radius expanded: the boulders in and around the river up to the cabin became my new adventure playground. The deep pools in the river became my swimming spot – when we weren't sneaking into the school pool at night, that is, or using the key to the home economics room that we'd been entrusted with, to steal ice cream and currant buns, which we gigglingly guzzled, far too fast, in the girls' loos.

A lot of my energy was channelled into the Holmedal Youth Group. We wrote, sewed, applied make-up, rehearsed and performed revues and other small plays without having a clue how lucky we were to have this kind of creative outlet.

Sometimes I wonder how my life would have panned out if I'd grown up today – or in a city, without all that free, wild, accessible outdoor space to romp around, in a childhood almost entirely dominated by the digital world.

I left lower secondary school with top marks in seven subjects. Yet I often say that I only learned two things in my last three years of compulsory education: how to forge my mother's handwriting and how to get good grades.

I was bright enough to cherry-pick which tests I needed to revise for, which classwork to prioritise and which lessons to do most preparation for. But above all I was lucky. I had the kind of willpower that made it possible for me to sit still and study.

As a result, I wasn't especially rowdy in class, the way many restless children are. My voice certainly made itself heard in the classroom, but I managed to use it in a reasonably constructive way. And if I bluntly refused to iron floorcloths in home economics because I thought they worked just as well un-ironed, my exam results were so good – and counted for so much more in the marking system than the classwork – that I got good overall marks all the same.

People who aren't able to use this restlessness constructively are generally diagnosed with ADHD. As an adult, I have also been tested. Although I tick many of the boxes – fidgeting, restlessness, excess energy – my concentration is too sharp, I'm too good at sitting still, and my recall is too clear for anyone to dare put the diagnosis in writing.

The diagnosis that best matches my reality

might be 'Inattentive ADHD', which is often associated with girls. Even though more boys than girls are diagnosed with ADHD, the condition can also affect girls, albeit often in a slightly different way – they tend to be less disruptive and more introverted. They may struggle just as much with concentration but compensate by daydreaming rather than acting up. This sort of behaviour is less of a nuisance in a classroom and so more difficult to pick up on. Although girls only account for 2 per cent of children with ADHD diagnoses, there are grounds to believe that the dark numbers are higher.

The first time somebody suggested I might have ADHD, I was surprised because the thought had never before crossed my mind. But now it makes sense of lots of things: for instance, when I was at upper secondary school, I had to ask for special permission to knit during class to help me concentrate; and nowadays, when I'm stressed and a bit tired after a long day at the office, it's better for me to go for a jog than lie down on the sofa. That lets me work all the twitchiness out of my body and feel calmer.

But is this a diagnosis of a behavioural

condition, or is it that society forces me and many other people into movement patterns we aren't designed for?

I'll leave that question hanging. I don't have a definitive answer. But diagnosis or not, the fact that I can cram facts into my head doesn't mean that I got any pleasure out of the theory-driven school system. I crammed for cramming's sake, for the marks; I crammed just enough to make sure the information stuck until the exam was over, but not a minute more – and then my goal was to forget it all. (In German grammar, for example, I counted how many times I needed to repeat a sequence of prepositions in order for it to stick, and if I then repeated it half as many times again, I could be fairly certain I'd remember it until the next day.)

Again, I was lucky that I could pull off this trick. There were others who were just as motivated as I was, but less able to deal with rote learning. They didn't get the same results and that sometimes felt unfair.

We constantly hear stories like this, about all the people who slip through the cracks at schools

focused on memorising facts. These are important, sad, powerful stories, and justify the claim
that the education system in Norway, in common
with many other societies, is too heavy on theory.
But Norwegian schools aren't just unsuitable for
people who are supposedly weak on theory. Rote
learning feels unfair and inappropriate for people
like me too. First of all, being given facts and
information in the abstract felt alien – I struggled
to find any relevance and grasp the point of what
I was learning. Secondly – and just as significantly
– I missed out on the chance to develop practical
skills. It didn't occur to me that I could be creative
not just with my mind, but with my body too, if
I put in the time and energy.

This is perhaps the greatest loss. And I can't
imagine it being a greater loss for a person who
is good at theory than someone who isn't. But
there is, of course, still hope. Taking a practical
course as an adult, chopping down trees, milking
cows and convincing myself I can build a privy
– all of this helps make up for what I missed. I
am still learning. Everybody can learn. It's never
too late.

The spruce must fall

At agricultural school, I wasn't a farmer (yet), but I finally got to use my whole self, hands and all. I also got to hone my skills using tools I scarcely believed I'd be able to master at first. One of them was the chainsaw.

It would be an exaggeration to say that working with the chainsaw appealed to me at once. For one thing, it was impossible to get hold of a pair of protective boots small enough for my size 36 feet and I felt like a clown wading around in the over-sized, over-clean protective clothing. The helmet and visor felt absurd when faced with the tiny willow twigs on which we started our training.

First we learned to make a directional notch, where you saw an open triangle that faces in the direction in which you want the tree to fall. Then, from the other side of the tree, you make a felling cut through the trunk at roughly the same height (preferably slightly above, never below), cutting straight through towards the notch until a five-to-eight-centimetre hinge remains. If the centre of gravity is right, the tree will then fall over the directional notch and the hinge will snap just before the tree hits the ground. You can help it along by driving wedges into the felling cut and tipping the tree in the correct direction.

We were also encouraged to make friends with the killing machine in our hands. You don't need to have seen *The Texas Chain Saw Massacre* to understand that a lot can go wrong with a jagged, razor-sharp saw chain hooked up to a petrol motor. And the more afraid you are of the saw, the further away from your body you hold it, the weaker you get – and the more dangerous it becomes.

I felt stupid and clumsy for a long time. Right up until the day it all went wrong, in fact. It was a pretty big spruce, and I lost control of the saw, cutting into the hinge. I realised I had to get out of the way, but had no idea just how fast I needed to move. Luckily, my teacher was right beside me. He virtually lifted me clear, just before the tree landed right on the spot where I'd been standing. Thanks for that, Marco.

The experience left me scared for a while. Rather than daring to tackle a trunk again, I turned into one of the people who went around stripping off the branches, which is about as boring as you can get. It couldn't end this way. I wanted to get back on the horse. When I turned thirty a few months later, my mother gave me a chainsaw, and then there was nothing for it but to give it another try.

Nowadays, after so much practice, the chainsaw is an extension of my hands. I know which sound means that I can't push it any further, and I know how to attack branches that are stuck in the ground so that the saw won't get caught between the branch and the trunk, and jam. My saw, a Husqvarna 445, has become a workmate I respect rather than fear.

So finally it felt like it was time to take a shot at that big, heavy tree.

That morning, the first thing I do is climb up with a rope, tie it tight, pull it across the clearing I've carved out and tie it firmly to another tree. Then comes the directional notch. Beforehand, I've measured roughly how far into the trunk I need to cut – about a quarter of the way. I carefully make sure that the bottom cut is parallel to the ground and make some fine adjustments. It's a good feeling, being able to use this brute of a machine to remove precisely those millimetres you're after.

Once I start on the felling cut, there's no way back. The tree trunk is thicker than the length of the chainsaw blade, so I have to stick the saw straight in on one side, parallel to the hinge, and circle around the trunk, like a fan. Three times I stop to drive in wedges. That stops the tree trunk from settling on the blade and trapping it. I work my way around this side of the trunk. The tree is steady as a rock. I start to drive in the wedges. I bash and bash and bash. Nothing happens. The Sitka spruce has grown quickly, far too quickly: the timber is soft and the wedges simply seem to be sinking into the trunk. My pulse rate starts to climb. Did I saw straight the whole way round? I had to take the saw out to drive the wedges in – so did I fail to follow the same track? Could there be a wood chip inside there holding it back? I go in again with the saw – I poke about slightly at random here and there to get a sense of it, and all of a sudden, I find I've sawn through the hinge. I've only gone through at the midpoint of the hinge, fortunately, so there's no risk of the tree landing on me. But still, it's the one mistake I really shouldn't have made.

*

I venture round to the front of the tree and tug on the rope. Lean on it with all my weight. Nothing happens. It's like I have no strength at all. What now? I dare not go to bed with a half-felled tree outside my window. A text pops up from my aunt. She and a girlfriend are on their way to a nearby peak and wonder if I want to join them. I don't. But should I ask them to come here and help me? Not quite yet.

Can the sailor in me help the lumberjack? I need more force on the rope. Transfer of energy. If I make two loops in the middle of the rope and pull the end through a few times I should, in theory, increase the force with every round. I try, and it works: I haul in an entire half a metre.

Again, I check the wedges – they're looser and I drive them further in. Back to the rope again. And so it goes for a couple of rounds. I pull. Strike. Pull. Strike. And pull. Now I can't manage any more. My arms were long ago sapped of strength. I lean on the rope one more time, but don't feel as if anything is happening at all. Then I hear it: the sound of a tree starting to fall. Its branches sweeping through the branches of the other trees around it; the swoosh as the huge tree rushes through the air and, at last, the noise of the hinge snapping – always a great sound. Since I'm now standing on a slightly different side of the tree from usual – the place where it will land, in fact – there's a whisper of fear, but even weighed down by heavy protective shoes, it isn't hard to run away and I still manage to enjoy the sound of the fall.

It's all because of that feeling. The tree fell precisely where I wanted it to. That's one thing. The cabin is still standing. That's another. I managed it. Single-handedly, with my own hands and my own brand-new knowledge. That is the most important thing. The fact that I was the one who worked out what needed to be done. Big, heavy tree versus small, newly trained woman ended in an away victory. I'll be damned if I'm not David, standing here gazing at the tree lying vanquished on the ground with my hands in the air like a champion no one sees.

TWO

*In which I convince myself I can make
a small but very useful building*

It's getting lighter around my cabin. Every tree I fell lets a bit more sunshine through to the red cabin walls. Inevitably, my project of clearing up after the planting frenzy of the post-war years is taking a lot longer than I'd imagined, but the light motivates me to press on. And one day, I clear my first gap in the trees, down towards the river that runs 20 metres below the cabin. Not only does this open up the view to the hills and mountains opposite, it also puts me in contact with the river in a way I wasn't before. Nice.

The trees are planted densely, and that's why there are so many of them. I make a point of clearing away all the branches and timber from each felled tree before making a start on the next – I've seen how chaotic it can get if you leave that sort of stuff lying around: the branches get tangled up in one another and soon it becomes impossible to tidy up anything at all. It's best to get it out of the way as you go along.

Working this way, I manage to fell three or four large Sitka spruces in a single day. Now there are branches in a big heap measuring around 20 cubic metres, as well as a couple of other smaller piles. I'd planned for the lumber before I started. But what I hadn't factored in was how much space it would take up.

Of course, I'll put it all to use. Spruce isn't brilliant for fuel, but it'll do. I gradually learn how spruce burns: the wood blazes fast without much smouldering, but that makes it good for cooking. Regulating the temperature on the Ulefos woodburner isn't really much more difficult than controlling my induction hob at home (although it takes a lot longer to boil water).

Even so, the woodpile in front of the cabin is growing quicker than I can burn it. Much quicker. What am I going to do with all the logs? The two-kilometre stretch down to the road is too long, steep and rugged to make it worthwhile to have them transported out. Of course, I can move them further into the forest and just forget about them

– they'll probably have composted within a couple of decades.

But they are energy. Power and strength. In one way or another, they could become a resource.

If only I weren't so bad at carpentry, perhaps I could build something. And that's when I start to think that I will have to face one of my big fears: to build something – and possibly fail on the way.

You can live on a knife and a branch

A couple of years ago, I took it into my head to go to folk high school. Faced with a whole range of practical subjects to choose from, and free to pick whichever I wanted, I settled on woodwork. And loathed it.

We whittled, chopped and planed knives, spoons, bowls and cups. Sandpaper was as good as banned: the aim was to learn to wield the knife and axe so precisely that there was no need for sanding. There are good reasons for this: sandpaper exposes all the cells on the surface of the wood, making it vulnerable to water, fungi and all sorts of harmful intruders, whereas the blade of a knife, axe or plane does the exact opposite: it seals and protects the surface.

That's assuming you master the technique, of course. For me it felt like an insuperable task to get the knife to move in those long, controlled strokes that it took to avoid notching and splintering the wood I was working. This incredibly painstaking work didn't suit my limited patience, especially when I was surrounded by a group of nineteen-year-olds who seemed, to me at least, to be cracking the technique without even trying.

I had the sense that only perfect was good enough. It felt impossible to start on anything before I knew how to do it – and of course it was impossible to know how to do something without getting started.

And what is perfect anyway? Is it even a desirable goal? I was full of doubts about what I could achieve. I realised that I needed to stop seeing others' achievements as an obstacle and find something or somebody I could learn from instead. As a person who wants to do so much, but dares so little, I needed to talk to someone about the difficulty of beginning and the impossible things we may still be able to achieve. I needed inspiration.

*

My quest takes me on a trip to Bø, a small college town in central Norway, some 150 kilometres southwest of Oslo, in the foothills of the mountains of Telemark. One rainy day, beside a river on the outskirts of the town, I find what I am seeking in a small wood workshop called Krokvokst (Crooked Grown). In the workshop sits Mari Fallet Mosand, carving a *krympeboks*, or shrink box – a wooden box made by hollowing out a log or branch and inserting a pre-dried base, then allowing the green, hollowed-out branch to dry around the base so that it becomes sealed. Mari has completed an order of ten boxes, which will be used as recruitment rewards for a craftwork group. Although all the boxes are made in the same way, they aren't identical. Nor are their surfaces smooth. It is easy to see the path of the knife.

Mari is one of the tiny minority of people in Norway who make a living from whittling. In the workshop of her one-woman business there are bentwood boxes, candlesticks, bread platters, bags and dishes made of willow, hazel and bulrushes, shrink boxes, ladles and knives and salad servers, stools and chairs. There are axes and knives and a shaving horse and home-made chairs and a radio that can play audiobooks. This is how Mari mostly works: with an axe, a knife and the green wood she has found in the forests of Bø.

The craft she practises doesn't really have a proper name, nor is there any formal training or certificate of apprenticeship for it – because in the days when everything people needed for house and home was whittled, shaped and hewn, this was something everybody could do. Maybe you could call it rural crafts. In Swedish, it's called *hemslöjd*, or handicraft.

Nowadays, almost nobody whittles their own spoons. Mari is one of the few people versed in the craft. And the knife marks left on the boxes, spoons, ladles and knives she makes are, in part, an illustration of her clear notions of what is and isn't perfect.

'If there are knife marks on my boxes, that's totally intentional. I think it's better to look at imperfection – it makes people happier,' Mari says.

For her, the perfect square drawn with a ruler is totally dead. It doesn't exist in nature because nature is always slightly askew, and we humans are nature too, after all.

It makes sense. As does the reason why Mari doesn't use sandpaper: she wants to be true to the craft, and for her that means showing that a human is behind it.

'I try not to smooth things over.'

In one of the boxes, Mari hits a knot in the wood. She turns the box over and over, feeling her way forward with the knife, then turns it again. She has to approach it from the right side, the side the material wants to be carved from, has to follow the direction in the fibres to achieve a smooth cut. Only then will it be any good.

Because of course, it must be good. But she's after quality, not perfection. This is Mari's regular work now. But she also started somewhere. She trained as a teacher and used to live in a big empty house in Bergen. She had no money, so she started making the things she needed.

'It was tremendously liberating,' she says.

For several years, Mari worked with wood in her spare time. She learned birch-bark plaiting, in part from her mother, and how to make a shrink box, at teacher training college. But the arts of whittling, wood-bending and other methods of shaping green, crooked, local wood into useful tools are things she has increasingly discovered on her own and bit by bit.

Then she had children and her spare time vanished. She realised that if she was going to create, she would have to do so during her working hours. Eventually she became a full-time maker.

It hasn't made her rich. As the only person in Norway to live off whittling, she makes ends meet. While she spends 70 per cent of her time in the workshop and 30 per cent as a course tutor, those percentages are reversed when it comes to income. But she is being true to herself.

'I have to create. And I think a lot of other people also have the same need,' Mari says.

I get a strong urge to stick up my hand. Me! I feel the need to create. And ever since I met Mari, I've taken great pleasure in the rough-hewn wooden spoon I eventually managed to whittle in the carpentry workshop at folk high school. I've even whittled another one. And I bought my own spoon knife (a knife with a round blade you use to carve out a hollow in the wood – it looks a bit like the tool people used to make butter balls in the

1980s) and made a teeny-weeny cup out of a burl. I keep salt in it, so it gets used every day.

What all these items have in common is that they mean a lot more to me than any of the spoons and bowls I've bought. They also remind me of a rather wise expression I once heard: if something's worth doing, it's worth doing badly first. Obvious, but good to keep in mind.

Now, the idea ripens. Maybe I can manage to build something with all this timber lying around the cabin after all.

In fact, there's a building I need. A very basic building that even a cabin as simple as mine could do with. When I was little, the loo at the cabin was a truly vile and pretty scary bucket toilet in the cellar. Dark and foul-smelling, it got chucked out the instant I took over, never to return – I'd rather use the river or dig a hole among the trees.

These methods are fine if I'm only up here now and then. But I want to spend masses of time here. I need an outdoor toilet. I don't need it to be big, and I'm not especially demanding when it comes to comfort and interior design. Nobody is going to spend long in there anyway. I can hide it in the trees.

But most important of all, the aim is not to make it perfect. I don't even have the resources I'd need for that, because if I'm going to build it, I'll build it using what I have around me. I'm not going to carry loads of planks, panels and cement up here.

And what I have is rapid-growth, densely branched Sitka spruce. Soft trunks and loads of tough branches are pretty much the opposite of what you'd ideally choose to build with. But it costs me nothing and I have plenty of it, and I want to build a privy making the most of what I have to hand. Because this privy of mine will be a homage to doing one's best, learning from one's mistakes and pressing on.

A school for everybody – and for the whole body

So now I have a goal: I'm going to build a privy that's good, but not perfect, and the materials will come from my immediate environment. I start to plan almost straight away – and almost straight away, I see problems: should I *build* a door? Will it be gloomy in there without windows? What tools should I use? And last but not least: it seems out of the question to use the traditional Norwegian method for building log cabins – *lafting* – but how am I supposed to transform my cylindrical logs into flat planks?

Luckily, I realise that I won't have to answer all these questions before getting started. Most of them will work themselves out along the way. But the last two questions trouble me. After all, there's no electricity at the cabin and even if there were, it's not as if I have masses of equipment at my disposal. I've had a cordless drill on my wish list for ages and this is as good a reason as any to get myself one. The chainsaw, of course, came up here with me. But beyond that, I'll have to rely heavily on my axe, saw, knife and plane.

When I rummage through the cabin's tool cupboard, I discover that I have more tools on hand than I'd realised. There are four axes in varying sizes, plenty of knives, a couple of saws and a thoroughly worn-out old plane. But the tools are in poor condition. They're rusty and will need at least one round on a grindstone – which I don't have.

If I'm aiming to become the kind of person who works with axes and the like, I also want to be the kind of person who can take good care of her tools. If I'm going to make life difficult for myself, I plan to do it in style.

So I decide to take a tool-sharpening course. Because there is such a course – and what's more, it's held at a veritable stronghold of Norwegian craftsmanship: the Hjerleid Craft School in Dovre.

Course participants are supposed to bring along their own tools. For this reason alone, it already seems perfect: without sharp tools, there won't be a privy. But my hope is that the course will offer me something more. I wonder if there will be other participants who are spending their spare time on building projects that they feel are unachievable. Is there a community for this kind of thing?

I'll admit, I'm quite excited. As I drive over Strynefjellet and up through Gudbrandsdalen, my thoughts race: what kind of people travel to Dovre to take a tool-sharpening course? How good are they at it? I don't like being the worst. I've done a bit of tool-sharpening before, mostly scythes, and

I've had a go on the odd sheath-knife. But I've never properly got the hang of it.

In theory, I get it. The bevel – the edge, if you like, the part of the tool that will be sharpened – needs to have a certain angle. As a rule, it's somewhere between 22 and 30 degrees. More acute for a sharp sheath-knife, although if it's too sharp, the blade will get stuck in the wood. The angle of an axe blade is larger, but if it's too large, the axe won't be any good at cleaving or carving. You're supposed to grind it until you get a raw edge, until it kind of bristles and, in many ways, feels anything but sharp. But once this is done evenly along the whole length, the blade is fully ground.

Then it's time to switch to the whetstone, which will remove the raw edge and polish away the tiny notches left by the coarse grinding disc or blade.

On arrival at Dovre, I enter a huge space, a *lafting* hall, where two or three half-finished log cabins serve as the backdrop to the tool-sharpening course. My first mistake is to tell the course leader, Steinar Moldal, that I think the plane I've brought along is so rusty that it's beyond rescue. That's not the kind of thing you say in restoring circles, where the starting point is a principle that the rest of society would do well to heed: conserve as much as possible; replace as little as you can. Most things can be used and even more can be repaired. If only 15 centimetres of the log in the wall is rotten, replace only 15 centimetres, or perhaps 20. If only the surface of the plane's blade is rusty, polish only the surface.

The body of my plane is wooden and probably home-made. Since my grandfather was a blacksmith, it's even possible that he forged the blade himself. I can't deny that it would be fun to restore it. It takes a good few rounds with the rust remover, but in the end I manage to get the blade out and, after just one quick session with the polishing disc on the angle grinder, it already looks much better.

And then the blade needs sharpening. There are twelve of us spread out across the *lafting* hall, bent over angle grinders and whetstones. Most of the other people on the course are dedicated hobbyists. A couple are art and crafts teachers; they're among the few lucky souls who still have properly functioning craft and woodwork rooms. For it is no longer compulsory to have these facilities in Norwegian schools, and a survey carried out by Norwegian broadcaster NRK in 2019 showed that 10 per cent of schools don't have one at all, while many of those that still exist are underused. Only half of all art and crafts teachers have formal qualifications.[3]

Some of the participants on the course are wood-carvers, but none of them are remotely expert in sharpening steel. Nor am I. Before long I find myself wondering whether courses like this are even suitable learning environments for me. I don't have the patience to make mistakes, and I am getting irritated and almost angry: it's one thing to find the right grinding angle, but quite another to maintain it for the entire length of the surface.

I know I can't expect to do it perfectly first time, but it's bloody annoying all the same. Mostly because the way it makes me feel is all too familiar: clumsy. It's a silly and unconstructive feeling which I think may partly stem from my childhood, from my memories of how unfulfilling woodwork often was.

I remember how hopelessly clumsy my hands felt when they were supposed to be making a bentwood box: you were meant to slowly place a thin, wet piece of wood around a mould, then glue it and fasten it with clamps so it would dry in that shape. I realised it would never turn out right, or not right enough, because I had never done it before and would never do it again: we would only work on bentwood boxes for this single period of secondary school woodwork, and that was far too little time to get the hang of it.

Head and hands learn from each other

But does my limited experience as a child actually have anything to do with the frustration I experienced in shaping a bentwood box, or my difficulties now with sharpening a plane blade? Even in the olden days, children rarely got to do more than turn the crank on the grindstone, which was hardly a proper training.

Well, it's something to do with the fact that although you're never too old to learn, and although it's great that growing numbers of adults are going on tool-sharpening courses and beer-brewing courses and weaving courses to learn a craft, none of them can ever hope to learn the way they could have as kids. And that applies to learning with both head and hands.

We are used to thinking that our big, clever brain is what made us what we are today, and that's why our hands are so functional. It's hardly surprising we think this way, because our brain is pretty fantastic. It accounts for 2 per cent of our body weight and uses up around 20 per cent of our energy. Our cranial capacity – the volume of the interior of our cranium – is roughly twice the size of the brain of our close relative the gorilla.

And yet, one of the most remarkable things about us humans is just how immature we are at birth. We have a grasp reflex, as primates do, but it is too weak to be used for anything other than emotional attachment. We are unfinished on the inside too, blank slates: our heads are full of knowledge-hungry neurons, just waiting for us to fill them with information. And a good many of these neurons will learn from our hands.

The amount of space our various body parts

occupy in our brain mass is far from proportional to their size. Perhaps that isn't so odd. But while we can understand at once why the gluteal muscles don't require as much brain capacity as the tip of our tongue, we may be surprised by how large a share of the brain is assigned to our hands. If motor skills determined the size of our body parts, our mouths, eyes and noses would be large, but far from the largest: our entire body would fit into just one of our hands, with room to spare.

In sensory terms, it is hardly surprising that the lips and tongue make a strong showing, but our hands beat everything: measured by the skin that covers them, they are our largest sense organ. No other part of our body – neither the tip of a tongue, nor the head of a penis – can measure up to the vast sensory library we have at our fingertips.

This is exciting. Given how much space our hands occupy in our heads, could it be that the head doesn't just learn from the hands, but that it goes the other way too? How did we become what we are and how are we to nurture the enormous potential we possess? To find out more, I invite myself to the office of neuroscientist Per Brodal.

'The fact that so many of our brain cells are programmed to control our hands shows that our hands have an awful lot of options to start off with,' Per Brodal tells me. His books include the standard text on our central nervous system and he is interested in the fact that, just as hands would have been almost nothing without the brain, the brain would have been nowhere near what it is without hands either.

The choices our hands make in the early years of our lives ultimately form our fine motor skills, he tells me. If these motor skills are to become as good as they possibly can be, they have to be used and used early. Because the blank cells in our heads won't wait forever. We only have a few years in our childhood and youth to train them with movement before they're gone – and this unique chance to train our hands disappears along with them.

Fortunately, this doesn't mean that our brain volume diminishes immediately, but it does mean that this space is used for other functions. So since I spent twelve years sitting in school where, according to lecturer and author Egil Børre Johnsen, the focus on theory 'is greater today than it was in ancient Roman schools',[4] the neurons that are good at this kind of knowledge ended up occupying more space than the ones that help my hands to draw the knife steadily over a wooden surface or plan the construction of a three-dimensional structure.

I ask Brodal if he can explain to me how the use of our hands affects our brain. Preferably in terms that are as concrete as humanly possible. The conversation takes us back to the history of our evolution.

'Our hands and head have evolved in parallel. Our brain has grown and become better, more finely tuned, at the same time as we have developed greater sensitivity in our hands,' he says.

This development has taken roughly three million years. Our foremothers began to use tools. This meant they had to be able to plan and they needed to have the ability to work towards a goal over a long period of time. Eventually, they also needed to be able to explain the process to their sisters and brothers, not to mention their children.

This need is what ultimately became language – yet another uniquely human quality. We don't know precisely how language came about. Perhaps we initially learned by copying each other. Then we started to mime messages, which is distinct from copying in that it is a planned utterance. This development was made possible by a brain that coordinates movements and visual perception.[5]

As humans started to migrate, the ability to talk about our experiences became even more necessary. Flexibility became necessary too. Generalists came into their own. When we reached new territory, we didn't know what would face us when we opened our eyes in the morning. Was the ground covered in cold white powder? Had the water grown hard and solid? Or was the stream suddenly nothing but dusty earth? Would we need to run as fast as we could from a forest fire or sit quiet as mice so the bull bison wouldn't hear us? Exciting times, these, when humans learned that adaptability might be the most important trait they could carry forward in their history.

That is why we have generalist hands. Not specialised hooves, like the horse, an animal of the steppes; or climbing hooves, like goats, an animal of the mountains. We have hands that can do a bit of almost everything and a brain that has set aside a disproportionately large space for this manual work.

But, as I mentioned earlier, all this brain capacity doesn't last forever – as demonstrated by far too many sad southpaw tales: left-handed children who were once forced to write with their right hand sometimes ended up with poor fine motor skills in both hands. If they tried to go back to writing with their left hand in adulthood, it wasn't capable of much either. The fine motor skills window in their parietal lobe had closed.

'Our brain triples in weight over the first year of life,' Brodal tells me, 'and continues to grow until we are five or six years old.'

Over these years, the neurons in the brain build connections – known as synapses – which eventually control our repertoire of movements for the rest of our life. Each cell becomes linked to hundreds or thousands of others.

Brodal explains that when they measure brain activity during various actions, scientists can see differences in how experienced a person is at performing an action. To begin with we use a big chunk of our brain to do something. We concentrate so intensely that a large part of our cerebral cortex literally lights up. As we become better and eventually really good at performing the action, the light goes out. Once the action is automatic – or overlearned – it has acquired a fixed place in our cerebral cortex. One example of this is tool use. If we are really good at it, the tools also sit in our brain – like an extension of our hand.

'There are no short cuts here. There are a lot of connections to be made,' Brodal emphasises.

Again, the early years of life are especially important. Our society works on the basis that there are critical phases for other senses and actions: children are expected to have a certain language level before the age of five, for example. Our hands probably have this kind of critical phase as well, but it isn't as strictly defined. Yet.

'We need to enable children to explore the world as fully as possible. Nurture their physical senses, especially in the face of constant growth in technology,' concludes Brodal. And his conclusion takes us, inevitably, to the school system.

An impractical education

We certainly don't know everything about human development, but what we do know is this: that our hands need at least as much stimulation and training as our minds to become good; and that the two are inextricably linked.

Based on this knowledge, we build a curriculum. Norway's compulsory education runs from years one to ten, followed by three or four years of optional upper secondary education. That is at least thirteen years under a state-run pedagogical superstructure. Right now, it is governed by Knowledge Promotion – the most recent educational reform.

The guiding principle behind Knowledge Promotion was to make teaching more targeted and reinforce the skills (or proficiencies) that are deemed to be fundamental. Norwegian pupils were judged to be not good enough at reading, writing and arithmetic, which left them lagging behind in all learning: if you can't read, you can't learn science either.

The four fundamental skills are the ability to express oneself verbally, read, write and use digital tools.

Digital skills are defined, among other things, as 'gathering and processing information, being creative and inventive with digital resources, and communicating and interacting with others in digital environments'.

This is all well and good and important. But what if we replaced 'digital' with 'physical' in the above paragraph? Wouldn't that reveal an essential part of what it is to be human, a part that can be developed or suppressed depending on how much stimulation it receives – in the school system, for example? Given everything we know about when and how children develop their motor skills, I mean?

There is little doubt that 'more practical learning in schools' has been a rallying cry among education officials for some time. The main or 'general' segment of the curriculum states that the system must 'train both hand and mind', instilling a 'desire to break new ground'.[6] But how much importance should we actually attach to recent efforts to increase practical learning in schools while their foundations continue to be so – indeed, are so fundamentally – theoretical and abstract, paying so little attention to the fact that we are physical beings with a physical urge to create?

The politicians appear to be trying to move from words to action – literally. The Ministry of Education and the civil service have reviewed and updated the entire curriculum in recent years, and one of their aims was to increase practical learning.

In 2016, the Education Minister at the time, Torbjørn Røe Isaksen, announced that he wanted to split art and crafts in two: one path would cover more theoretical art and aesthetics, while the other would cover practical craftwork. Pupils would have to choose between these two subjects. And from autumn 2020, vocational craftwork became available as an optional course in secondary school.

The key word here is 'vocational'. The new subject is intended to recruit pupils for vocational study at upper secondary level – and on into working life. Again, all well, good and important – but does this mean that only those who pursue craftwork as a profession will be able to develop their practical side? It's not as if we can't afford to give everybody this opportunity.

In fact, this argument was used to justify the

changes in the teaching of art and crafts: 'Manual dexterity and a capacity for practical problem-solving are vital general skills for everyday life,' wrote the working group.[7]

That is how simply, how correctly it can be put. And the outcome ought to be a new, fundamental skill: whether practical, physical or creative.

Because manual dexterity is also a skill, and practice and practical knowledge are not simply tools for getting restless children to sit still and absorb more theoretical knowledge – they are an end in themselves. Even in a world where digital skills are paramount, practical skills are still required.

Back at the tool-sharpening course, the plane blade becomes sharp in the end. First of all, I grind it straight on a belt grinder, then concave on a whetstone and then I start to hone the back. You see, it has to be straight – flat – and that is easier said than done. Finally, the angle grinder comes out to do its bit.

We put the plane back together again, and I'll be damned if it doesn't sing when I test it out on a log that's lying around. I'd never realised before that planes sing. Suddenly, I think courses are cool again.

And I travel home, boot crammed with sharp tools: axes, knives, the plane and even a scythe. On my side of the mountain I meet the spring. Now, there are no more excuses, only suspense, anticipation, curiosity and the urge to create: there's building to be done.

THREE

*In which I climb on something
I have built myself*

Back at the cabin, everything is a bit more difficult, of course. I puzzle and think and ponder, and look at logs and plots of land: where should the privy stand – how far away from the cabin? How am I going to get it built and where do I start? I mean, how am I supposed to anchor it to the ground?

I already know that the soil is full of rocks. After all, it's just metres from where the river runs – the river that carved out much of the valley here after the ice retreated. That kind of thing leaves a fair number of rocks. On top of that, the spruce trees have spread a thick, even layer of roots across the entire surface – around, between and under the rocks.

Even so, I want to dig. I want to build the privy on posts that are sunk into the ground. Since I have so much material to choose from, I've decided that my corner posts might just as well be pretty oversized. If I can just get the holes dug deep enough, the surrounding stones and roots will help keep the posts in place – I hope. Then I'll build a framework around them, brace them against each other with diagonal bracing, build a floor and a roof, install a seat with a round hole in it and fix cladding on the walls. It's a doddle, and all doable in a single afternoon, if you look at it that way.

Of course, if you take a closer look, you immediately see an endless series of challenges. Not only will I have to shift some pretty big rocks, the posts will be heavy too. They'll need to stand reasonably straight, both individually and in relation to each other. Is this something I can do on my own?

That is something I'll never find out. Because I ask for help. Jakob is an Austrian friend who has a fair amount of construction experience. He happens to be on holiday nearby with a fellow Austrian called Konni. They both seem to think that helping build a privy in the Norwegian mountains is a suitably exotic way to kill a weekend.

The trees have been felled, the logs chopped and stripped of branches. The site has been selected – around 50 metres from the cabin, shel-tered in my small forest on a reasonably flat spot in a nice little clearing.

Our work starts with a pot of coffee on a campfire, and some paper and a pencil, so that we can work out what each of us needs to do.

The campfire won't only be used for coffee-making, though. I also want to singe the bases of the corner posts in the flames in the hope that the charred surfaces will protect them against rot. It's a trick I learned from fence-building. Spruce isn't exactly prized for its durability, but charred posts should be able to stand for thirty to fifty years at least. Time will tell whether or not my method works. That's the way it is with this whole venture, really: I may be able to get things to stand upright and stay together for now, but only time will tell how well they'll hold up, how it will all work.

But first, there's digging to be done – with a spade, a pickaxe, a crowbar and that excited enthusiasm you always get in the starting phase. The rocks are big and densely packed, but not so big and densely packed that they're any match for our tremendous zeal. Roots split in two as the pickaxe and axe force their way through. Sooner than any of us imagined, we have dug four metre-deep holes in the earth.

The only question is whether it's all happened a bit too fast. We carry up the posts and put them in the holes, one after another. But the square they make doesn't look totally square, so to speak. More like a rhomboid, or maybe mostly a bit wonky. A fair share of the blame lies with the big rocks. They force us to move the holes and we don't always have a chance to choose for ourselves where they will go. But our own eagerness is also a factor: we've been a bit too keen to get the holes over and done with so we can start on the actual building.

So what are we to do now? If we dig new holes, they'll end up overlapping with the ones we've already dug. After all, they're a good half a metre in diameter and the planned length of the walls is no more than a metre or so.

No, they'll have to do. We launch ourselves into fixing the corner posts: deal with them one by one, position them in the holes, measure with a spirit level, pack pebbles and larger stones and earth and turf around them. Stomp and jump and slam with a sledge-hammer to make it more compact, then hammer extra rocks into the earth. Each post must stand upright on its own, and they all do eventually, but they won't have any strength or stability until we fix them together. They are still wobblier than I think a good fence-post should be before the netting is attached.

But Jakob thinks they're good enough and, although he's only in his early twenties, he's helped build more houses than I have. He and his father are completely renovating an old smallholding together. What's more, he's taking what sounds like a really smart course in Graz, a combination of engineering studies and architecture. We met on a sailing trip a couple of years back. Jakob is one of those all-round nice guys. Even on a sailing boat, where space, food and heat are in short supply, it's impossible to be irritated by him. He's exactly the kind of person you'd want to build a house with.

So we do. The posts are upright, and now it's out with the drill, some extra-long screws and some slightly thinner poles to hold the corner posts together. And this is where things really start to get exciting. Not that there's anything wrong with hand tools, but a fully charged drill is just so much fun. It's a useful tool to master: 15-centimetre screws simply vanish into the wood, and with every new pole that's added the structure holds up better. Before we start, I can move each post simply by shaking it with one hand. Once they are fastened together in pairs, I have to use two hands. Now that all four posts are attached to each other, the whole structure feels perfectly steady. But we still add diagonal bracing here and there too, plus frames for the door and window, before we dare to truly test the construction. And we do this by climbing up on it, of course.

However much I've loved climbing in the past – trees and rock faces and sailing-boat rigging and siloes – I've never loved it as much as I do now, clambering up a climbing frame I've built myself. Because once we've started to attach the rafters but haven't yet begun to add the roof planks, the structure really is a perfect climbing frame. You can hang and dangle from it, climb up and down and around and over and through it, and it doesn't shift so much as a millimetre. The poles, which are only partly stripped of bark, offer good friction and feel totally secure. One day I'm going to have to build one of these just to play on.

But this one, unfortunately, must have a roof added, and once there are planks on the rafters, its climbing value diminishes. Even so, the mood is good. The sun is shining and the late-summer heat still lingers enough for us to enjoy feeling nice and cool amid the spruce trees.

Of course, I could – and perhaps should – have interlocked the logs, using traditional notching techniques. But although that might have made it stronger and more beautiful, it would also have taken a whole lot more time. Right now, I think it looks rough around the edges and cool. I'm enjoying the progress, the pace and the company. We work well together and it's fun to show off my cabin and its surroundings.

'How did your grandfather get these enormous stones so neatly positioned in the foundation wall?' Jakob asks, and I feel extremely guilty. For me, the cabin has just always been there – a place where we've spent weekends and holidays for as long as I can remember, and I've never given any thought to how it came into being. Now, of course, I start to wonder myself. If the log cabin was ready-made when my grandfather 'won' it, it must have been carried up here in sections and mounted on the foundation wall. How did he get it all into place? And what about the big cast-iron wood-burner in the kitchen? How did they get that up here – without a helicopter, I mean? The entire foundation wall is built of huge natural boulders, probably from the river, laid precisely as they need to be to make the wall stable. How did he do that?

I know my grandfather was fond of stone. One of my favourite stories, which I like partly because I don't know quite which bits to believe, is about just that: Grandfather Steinar and a stone. The rock in question is actually in the river directly below the cabin. It is roughly 2 metres long, 1 metre wide and 1.5 metres high, and split in two lengthwise. It's divided pretty much perfectly down the middle along its length, the two halves leaning against each other with a gap in between.

But this rock hasn't always been split. The story goes that my grandfather devoted a great deal of time and effort to trying to split it – quite why isn't entirely clear, but he probably intended to use it somewhere. He tried his luck with hand tools and dynamite. The story goes that he still hadn't abandoned hope of splitting that rock by the time he died rather abruptly of a stroke in 1971.

Not long after my grandfather's death, there was a storm in Holmedal. Thunder and lightning. It happens now and then, but it isn't often that the lightning finds its way straight down between the mountains. But that evening it did. Lightning struck the river, and the rock, and split it in two. The way it now lies. The way my grandfather wanted it to be split.

I'll say no more. But I'll probably never get closer to the grandfather I never met than up here at his cabin.

Now that I start to look for it, I can see signs of my grandfather's industry all around me. The trees stand in straight rows. According to my father, it was no fun at all planting them, but that was the kind of thing people were expected to do when Norway was being rebuilt after the war. My grandfather dug deep ditches between the trees, intended to help the spruces thrive in this boggy terrain. In some places the ditches pass between the rocks, and in others I see that huge rocks have been moved. Out of the ditch and in under the cabin.

Not everything is quite up to scratch. In the kitchen, there's a sink with an outlet pipe, but the water just runs straight out into a bucket that I have to take outside to empty. The practical work and know-how ended with my grandfather. When I inherited the cabin after my father's death in 2006, it was pretty run-down. The slates were rotten, the panelling clearly hadn't had the painting it needed. There was no putty in the window frames and not all of the windows would have closed again if you'd opened them. I didn't want to sell the cabin, but wasn't interested in fixing it up and, besides, I didn't live close enough to do it myself. The solution was to lend it to a carpenter who agreed to do the work in exchange for use of the cabin. I paid for the materials. The cabin got new cladding, new double-glazed windows and a new corrugated-steel roof with rock wool insulation. When I took it back over, it was ready for a new generation.

The roof packed with practical maths

Jakob and Konni have gone home and I'm all alone with my structure. It doesn't take long for now-me to become irritated with past-me's lack of precision.

The fact is, my privy definitely isn't square: the angles aren't so far off that you'd notice it from a distance, but now, when I'm about to add a window, door and roof, I notice it. A lot.

As soon as we laid the roof boards, we found out just how wonky the building was. One of the side walls is 15 centimetres longer than the other. As a result, the lowest roof boards had to be sawn off at a slant. The last board was just a small triangle down in the corner.

I'd had these boards lying around here and there – some in the cellar, some old and some left over from when the cabin was fixed up. We'd laid them tightly together side by side, and I stretched a tarp over the top. The tarp has stayed watertight, but now it's time for it to be taken off and a metal roof – corrugated steel – to be put on.

The corrugated-steel roof is also a leftover from the renovation. Originally, the cabin was shingled with rounded slates but so many of them had become so rotten that the carpenter who fixed the place up didn't dare put them back on again. I still have the slates stacked up. To start off with, I thought I'd use them on the privy roof. But then the practical challenges presented themselves: I don't have any battens to lay the slates on, I don't know how to lay them and it'll take a lot more time than just whacking on a couple of steel sheets.

At least, that's what I think initially. In an ideal world, the steel roof should also be laid on battens, of course, just like the slates, to prevent damp and rot getting into the planks beneath. But my privy is a fairly airy construction, so it'll just have to do without. There's still one challenge left, though: the steel sheets are longer than the roof. How am I going to cut them to size?

Normally, I'd use an angle grinder. But I don't own one, I have no power to connect it to anyway and buying myself a cordless one just to cut a couple of steel sheets to size feels expensive and extravagant. I don't have a hacksaw or any other metal saws either. In the end, I decide to use the sledge-hammer and the rusty, blunt axe in the cellar. A couple of blows and I break through the steel. First of all I hack through all the corrugations that bulge in one direction, then I turn the sheet over and deal with the ones that bulge in the other. Beautiful it ain't, but it works – and I can always get hold of a hacksaw later.

The surface of the roof is small enough for me to get the sheets up there easily, but too large for me to stretch over and fix the screws in the middle without climbing on it. It's pretty steep, but fortunately not so steep that I can't sit on it.

Just how steep is it? That's a handy thing to know about a roof, whether in more formal buildings where different types of roofing are required to have different pitches, or in my case, where it will tell me, among other things, whether or not the snow will slide off.

We can calculate the pitch of the roof as an angle – the angle between the lowest back wall and the highest front wall. Or as the relationship between the length of the wall and the height difference between the two walls – a percentage.

Which way do you suppose it's easiest to measure this?

Hey presto! All at once, quite without thinking about it or even especially dreading it, we're caught up in maths. Caught up in Pythagoras, sines, cosines and tangents – terms that send me right back to upper secondary school, when I wore out two maths teachers in a single year.

I had opted for the music programme, but we were still expected to take lessons in some non-vocational subjects, including a year of maths. The maths lessons came when I was seventeen, pretty demotivated, extremely obstinate and armed for battle – my weapon of choice being the question 'Why?'

Over the course of the year, we were supposed to learn about things like sines, cosines and tangents, the magic formulae for calculating how many degrees there are in the angles of right-angled triangles. But we weren't expected to become especially good at maths. We needed to learn just enough to be able to study Gender Theory, Middle Eastern History or Social Anthropology, in case we chose to abandon a musical career and go to university instead – although not enough to embark on an engineering or nursing degree. So we weren't going to learn why it functioned the way it did, just how to work out the answer on the calculator.

My head refused to accept this. I'm incapable of learning anything from a rule I'm simply supposed to follow. I need something concrete to anchor the knowledge, an understanding of why it is the way it is. I was frustrated that my maths teachers couldn't give me that – and I made no effort to keep my frustration to myself: on the contrary, I pounced on any opportunity to berate them about the impossibility of accepting something I didn't understand. I can only apologise for that today. But I think my point still stands. Knowledge is understanding.

Including the compulsory maths lessons in primary and lower secondary school, I ended up studying the subject for ten years, but there's only one occasion I can remember truly getting anything out of the teaching: when the corridors and stairwells of my secondary school were due to be painted and my class was given the task of working out how much paint would be needed. All at once, hitherto abstract concepts like angles, area, geometry and percentages became concrete and useful – for a brief moment they were manageable. And then the walls were painted and the maths lessons returned to the foggy realms of abstraction.

My work on the privy has given me a chance to recover the feeling I experienced during that corridor-measuring exercise: my thoughts will happily take an extra turn around the right-angled triangles I'm dealing with, the measurements I'm taking, the mental arithmetic – not to mention the relationship between the different lengths and heights I have around me.

And if I turn back to the initial question – what's the easiest way for me to find the pitch of the roof? – of course it depends on what tools I have to hand, but also on how my head is put together: I do have a carpenter's rule and a measuring tape and even a try square, and these are good tools that I use all the time and with increasing confidence.

But I have my body too. So if I don't have a metre rule, I can use an arm instead. Knowing that there's a distance of 1.5 metres between the fingertips of my right and left hands when I stretch my arms out to either side isn't just a fun fact: I can put it to practical use.

*

In the evenings, I read in front of the fire – Jon Godal's *Å rekne brøk med han tykje* (*Calculating Fractions with Old Nick*). Godal is a researcher of traditions, famed for his fierce commitment to everything from old boats to old houses, as well as the associated craftwork. In this book, he talks about how calculation – mathematics – also has a place in cultural history and in the human body. His view is that even if the aim in mathematics is to obtain a definitive answer, a number is far from the only thing that can express the answer. The system of digits we operate with is no more naturally evolved than the rest of our language – it is just one language among many.

Godal's argument does me so much good. This is precisely what I need to understand in order to make the abstract concrete. My roof construction and those wonky loo walls of mine are teeming with trigonometric functions. But I don't need to know them.

The only thing I need to know is what Godal calls the 3–4–5 triangle.

Put simply, the method states that a right-angled triangle with sides measuring 3 and 4 has a diagonal of 5. This applies regardless of whether the numbers 3 and 4 are expressed in centimetres, feet, the length of your arm or a stick that you're holding. If the walls are 3 and 4 sticks long, respectively, the diagonal will be 5 sticks long if they meet at a right angle.

This idea is so much easier to grasp than sines, cosines and tangents that I almost feel cheated. What on earth was the school system playing at?

Craftspeople use this technique on a daily basis, to ensure that a building has four right angles, for example. If I had read the book a bit sooner – or more to the point, if practical, applied mathematics had been as central as the theoretical variant in my maths education – I would have been better equipped to make right angles in my privy.

Ultimately, like so much else, it's all about the golden mean, achieving a balance. It's not that we need to throw away books and pens and calculators. But it would be helpful to acknowledge that this is just one approach, and that we could benefit from using our bodies to achieve a full understanding of mathematics.

Now let's combine this perception of mathematics as a theoretical subject with the general underappreciation of the practical trades: who is best at mental arithmetic – an accountant with a desk and a screen full of calculators, or a sheet-metal worker who would have to put down their welding equipment and take off their gloves and visor to access any tool other than their head to calculate an angle, a distance or a height?

How do we know what we need to know?

Knowledge in action. Could we make more use of it? The Norwegian Correctional Service has tried in various ways, including a research project entitled 'It's the small steps that count: increasing knowledge about practice-orientated teaching of basic skills in the correctional service'.[8]

Prisons run schools at all levels and they also offer work programmes. In this project, the two were simply combined: courses in elementary skills became a component of the work programme in six selected prisons. In one prison, mathematics was linked to the design of wooden products in the workshop – using measurements, writing up schedules and calculating product pricing and material costs. At another prison, the project involved building a new teaching space in the woodwork room. By the end of this experimental course, four students obtained the vocational upper secondary school qualification in Construction Techniques and the programme was continued beyond the trial period. Other prisons linked teaching with car workshops, catering or cleaning duties.

The main benefit for the prisoners? A sense of achievement. 'If you don't get that, there isn't any point,' as one of the interviewees says. Another of the prisoners puts it like this: 'Yes, it gives you motivation, but it also creates images and understanding, making the theory easier to grasp. Because if I understand what I can use it for, I can find the motivation to learn it.'

Motivation, understanding and achievement. Given that these skills – practical skills – are precisely what Norway is most in need of right now, you might well wonder why it seems so difficult for society to successfully prioritise them.

A survey conducted by the Confederation of Norwegian Enterprise every four years to map the skills needed by its members shows that only

7 per cent of those businesses need to recruit staff with PhD-level qualifications. On the other hand, around half will need either craftspeople, engineers or other workers with technical qualifications within the next five years.

The number of people with PhDs in Norway has increased sevenfold since 1980, in a labour market that will need half of its employees to have vocational qualifications in future. Something, to put it mildly, is a bit off.

How did we end up here? Until the 1950s, the university system was developed based on forecasts of how many students society needed. This proved difficult and around 1960 there was a shift in the universities' focus, with an emphasis on education and research in the natural sciences, technology and sociology, with the aim of aiding the development of the welfare state.

At the same time, the first student boom kicked in: in a matter of years, student numbers increased by 50 per cent. This was costly, and the easiest solution was to restrict access to the most expensive subjects – medicine, for example – while cheaper subjects in the Humanities and Social Sciences faculties were easily accessible. Politicians probably didn't expect so many people to opt for courses that were completely divorced from working life – but they were wrong. Because people did. And unemployment rose.

Even so, throughout the 1990s, the government continued to think it was better for young people to be in education than jobless. Soon subjects that had once been small and niche became bigger than the traditional vocational subjects. You could no longer expect to get a teaching job at the end of your studies. The humanities, which had once served to train teachers, developed into disciplines that were largely focused on academic research.[9]

Today the pendulum is, perhaps, swinging back. At any rate, educational institutions, the authorities and organisations – both employer and student bodies – all wish to see a greater connection between university and working life, as well as more practice-orientated studies.

But as things stand, we will have a shortfall of 90,000 skilled workers by 2035. Will the measures be sufficient? I suspect not. Even though current efforts are the most substantial for several decades, we probably can't protect vocational subjects by focusing our efforts on them alone. We must also set up apprenticeships in companies. We must dispel the myth that vocational subjects are best suited to those who can't sit still, whereas people with good marks should opt for academic subjects, at the same time ensuring that those who struggle with theoretical knowledge in the current school system still have a chance to succeed in working life. We must embrace new technology – while preserving knowledge about raw materials and basic craftsmanship.

But first and foremost we must give everybody a chance to try. Nurture practical knowledge in everyone, so that those who want to can carry on, can make it a career path. Just as we do with theoretical knowledge, in fact. Imagine if we could place the two on an equal footing. What a world that would be.

And offering 'everyone' the chance to gain practical skills has to mean all genders. A more practical education can't be restricted to people who have dyslexia or find it difficult to sit still in class, and it can't be restricted to boys.

When Torbjørn Røe Isaksen unveiled his new two-path art and crafts programme in 2016, a national newspaper asked him if there wasn't a risk that boys would end up choosing craft and girls art. The then Minister of Education replied: 'There's a possibility you may get a degree of gender segregation but I think there's great value in choosing based on what you're interested in.'[10]

When a regional newspaper wrote a feature on Skills for Working Life courses and other practical subjects on offer in its city's schools, the head-teacher of Smiodden School said the following: 'Our optional subjects include the production of goods and services. Girls dominate, and have made bags and beauty kits, etc. Now we want to use part of the craft room to give boys a chance to do wood- or metalwork, or other similar things.'[11]

I'm sure both remarks were well intentioned, but it's a bit sad – and I think it pretty thoroughly misses the mark.

We are constantly told that the school system in Norway serves girls best. And yes – they do get higher marks and are seen as better at sitting still and not being disruptive in class, but girls also rank highest in another, much more dismal statistic: between 2008 and 2017, the use of antidepressants among girls aged 15 to 17 almost doubled. That is much larger than the increase among boys.[12] One in four teenage girls suffers from sleep problems, anxiety and stress. And girls are also the leading users of anti-anxiety medicine and antibiotics. Researchers don't know why these problems affect girls so much more.[13]

And that means I don't know either. But, based on my own experience as a girl with late-identified ADHD-like physical restlessness, I can speculate: the fact that girls don't cause a commotion with their unease doesn't mean it isn't there.

I've always been the kind of person who claims their space, so it's probably not obvious to everyone that I was one of those girls who sat there bottling things up. But I didn't let everything out in class – far from it – because the 'good girl' impulse regulated and controlled things and, besides, I had break-times and evenings to let off steam, by scaling buildings, partying or swimming in the fjord at midnight after a few too many drinks.

Although the theoretical rules for everything, from arranging a choral work to how the theme in

Bach's prelude was reversed and modulated, were understandable, they were also a pain in the neck. Why? What's the point of this? Fidget, fidget, twitch, prickle went my hands, feet and forehead, as my eyes drifted to the window. There, up on the hillside, I spy an excellent roof: the Co-op building – that'll be tonight's challenge.

How many other stressed girls are there sitting in Norway's classrooms keeping everything bottled up? Could there be some link between this lack of practical stimulation and girls' mental health problems? The question is too complex, too complicated, too large and too important for me to speculate unduly, much less draw any conclusions.

But a more practical school system and a more practical everyday life must not lead to more gender segregation. In the same way that more broad-based teaching would help pupils who are strong on theory as much those who are weak, so I believe that it can – and must – stimulate girls just as much as boys.

Girls have bodies too; we too are made to be in motion, to create and shape, to feel the sense of achievement that comes from making use of our hands.

In place first time

Yes, these are the kinds of thoughts that run through my head as I potter about by myself, tinkering with my privy. Yet the most important thing during these days at the cabin is my sense of achievement. I enjoy laying the roof and although it is hardly a textbook structure, I know it'll work. I get the corrugated-steel sheets in place, secure them using roofing screws with waterproof rubber washers and cut a length of metal which I hammer reasonably flat to form a flashing that I throw over the front of the roof at its highest point to make sure the water won't leak in underneath.

I pave the small floor space between the seat and the door with rocks. It took a while to work it out, but of course that's what I do – I have rocks all over the place after all. A few of them are even reasonably flat, though not all, and not all of them need to be: using some big and some small and some round and some sharp, I build a tiny little floor in my tiny little privy. Everything goes into it, everything is good for something and my floor ends up being stylish and functional.

Then I put in the window. The frame is in place

and the window is an old single-glazed one that also pre-dates the renovation. I level it out with wedges in the frame then screw it into position and, once it's firm, I place drip boards above and below – and I'm still only into the early part of day two.

Time to heave the door into place. It's really big and heavy. I settled on using the old cellar door. The original frame had totally rotted away and, besides, the cellar isn't in use because it's so full of junk. So for now, until I'm overcome by the urge to clear it up, I'll use the door here instead. I have some new hinges, one half of which I fix to the door-frame and the other to the door, then I lift it up, heavy as it is, and drop it straight in. First go. Not that I'm bragging.

FOUR

*In which I gather building materials
from nearby and weave a wall*

I am in love. Head over heels. With juniper wattle.

From the start of my privy project, I'd wondered if I could somehow clad the walls with juniper branches. There were certainly plenty of bushes on the boggy ground around the cabin, and surely the technique needed to attach them to the wall couldn't be that difficult. Juniper cladding has historical roots in this climate zone, if not exactly in my local area. I had seen and admired many enormous barn walls covered in the locally grown material, in Nordhordaland in particular. I understood that wattling must require an enormous amount of graft and effort, and was probably really team-work. But my walls were on a smaller scale, only about 1.5 metres wide and 2 metres high, and what's more, a couple of them had a door and a window, and the back wall, where the waste accumulates, would have a panel that could be unscrewed, in case the privy needed to be emptied at some point.

I had only ever seen the juniper-clad walls from a distance, so I got myself a book on roofing and cladding techniques using local materials, written by the same Jon Godal who had previously taught me about practical mathematics. The book included a twelve-page introduction to juniper wattle.

Would that be enough? Godal certainly has a lot to say on the subject and he sometimes feels almost like an atheist's household god, but I also had to be careful not to pay too much heed to him: he had so many rules that it started to sound difficult. I had to make sure I stopped reading while I still felt inspired, and not allow myself to be put off.

But I'm excited about juniper wattle from the word go. For once, I have the perfect raw material: juniper that grows on boggy ground. According to Godal, the bushes should be tall with long branches, so they can be pulled up from the ground, cut with branch cutters (which I actually have) and then woven into a wall with relative ease. The technique is time-consuming, but not particularly complicated.

First I have to make a kind of warp of horizontal battens – round, stripped branches – placed about 20 centimetres apart. The juniper branches are then woven in front of one batten, behind the next and in front of the third. The weave has to be tight, and I have to pay particular attention to the corners, to select branches with plenty of foliage so there's enough body to the wall. As Godal writes, with a twinkle in his eye, I should use branches that are 'suitably stiff and bushy'.

Before I can start weaving, I have to fix the battens in place. I decide to use spruce, as it's also something I have in abundance. Then I have the bright idea of using branches from trees that I've already felled. There are three piles of branches around the cabin that are in danger of becoming so high that it will soon be hard to add to them. Even with the vague hope that the weight of the snow in winter might compress them, every branch that doesn't need to be kept helps.

So I spend a morning chopping and stripping enough branches to make a warp for the first wall – the one I want to be made entirely from juniper, without any doors, windows or panels. The

113

branches are not straight, but they are pliable, so I should be able to sort that with a few screws and a drill, I think.

But I soon discover that it's not going to work. The branches prove to be so hard that there is no way I can get a screw through them. If I had thought about it, I might have realised sooner – I know that the twigs on a trunk are often much harder than the wood itself, but it hadn't occurred to me that the branches would be so unyielding. And now that I know, there's nothing for it – all I can do is swear, and start again.

I decide to use the trunks of small trees for my battens instead. Fortunately, there is no lack of raw material. It takes the whole afternoon, which is indescribably annoying, but I have to remind myself that I'm doing this for the first time and can't expect everything to go according to plan.

I eventually manage to get the battens in place and can start to gather the juniper branches. There is inevitably a bit of trial and error to begin with – I have no idea what makes for a good branch and what doesn't, but I realise pretty fast that I'll soon find out.

There's plenty of room and time for improvement. I listen to the radio as I weave. I carry on weaving. I have to inspect each branch, see how far I've come on the wall, and decide if it's usable. If it is, I'll still probably have to break or chop off a few twigs to make it 'suitably stiff', so that I can push and pull it into place on the wall. Physically, I can feel that it's hard work, but not so hard that I have to stop. I carry on for a long time.

And believe it or not, the work is varied. I carry the bundle of branches on my back from the mountainside to the privy. To do this, I lay a rope double on the ground, pile the juniper up, then pull the rope tight and heave it over my shoulder. I manage to carry enough in each bundle that the juniper starts to run out just as my arms are getting tired from the weaving. My arms then get the rest they need when I walk out to the juniper bushes with the branch cutters, because I've discovered that it's easier to cut than to pull up the bushes. As the privy is in among the spruce trees, it's sheltered from the wind, wet and cold that often meet you out in the open, and it's shady when the sun is too bright. And because the work is varied, I get to experience a bit of everything.

I'm creating; I'm active. My movements are meaningful. Is this a luxury in our modern world? Or a curse? I can certainly feel in my body that I've been moving in a way I'm not used to and that I've been working for a while; I can feel it in the muscles in my back, shoulders and feet, in my forearms. Is that a twinge of tendonitis I feel? Should I be worried, or will the pain literally make me stronger? Is it necessarily a bad thing to feel that I've been using my body?

We are made to move

On a small street in Trondheim, you will find what is perhaps the scariest piece of graffiti in Norway: '1 in 2 Norwegians walks less than 500 metres a day,' it says on the bridge over the railway tracks at the station. The graffiti was commissioned and approved by the public authorities. I gasp, wide-eyed. Is that really true?

It is. The figures are based on a Statistics Norway travel survey from 2015, which shows that 47 per cent of all Norwegians walk less than half a kilometre a day.[14] The few metres that we walk to and from the car are included. And if you think about it, it makes sense: our car is parked right outside our door, we drive to the nursery gate, to the garage under our office building, to the shop (or we might even have a meal delivered to our door), to our afternoon activities, and then the day is done. But is that how we want to be?

That is certainly not how we're put together. 'People are made to move,' it says in the introduction to the Norwegian Directorate of Health's 'Activity Handbook 2008'. Physical activity was once part and parcel of a 'demanding everyday life', whereas the lack of it today can lead to problems such as obesity and diabetes.

The report states that even though we are training and exercising more than ever before in our free time, this is still not enough to compensate for the loss of the positive effect that 'physical activity in daily life' once had. We need to use our bodies more consistently. If we all managed to do the minimum, not only would we benefit as individuals, the government would also save around 239 billion Norwegian kroner a year. By way of comparison, this is a good deal more than the oil income included in the 2018 national budget.

But it's impossible to get as much movement as we should in our free time. Between 30 and 50 per cent of us don't even manage to set aside 30 minutes for moderate physical exercise every day.

Work is nominally included in the Directorate's definition of physical activity.[15] And yet the Directorate of Health does not recommend a single initiative that involves work, either in its hefty professional handbook, or in its national guidelines and public advice.

Qigong, rowing and deep water running are included in its catalogue of physical activities, but normal manual activities such as clearing snow, picking blueberries or baking bread (when you knead the dough yourself) are not even mentioned.

One possible reason for this is that the Directorate of Health draws a distinction between sitting still and getting too little activity: 'With regard to recommendations for physical activity, measures to reduce time spent sitting differ from those needed to increase our activity level to moderate intensity.'[16] So we don't necessarily work up enough of a sweat while vacuuming to prevent the health issues that arise from not being active enough. That is typical health bureaucrat thinking.

The Directorate of Health is not alone in forgetting physical work when it comes to the need to move our bodies. When I googled 'How does physical work affect your body?' the answers I got were: 'This is what exercise does to your body' (*Verdens Gang* newspaper), 'The heart, blood vessels and exercise' (Norwegian Health Information) and 'Illnesses that can be cured with exercise' (*Dagbladet* newspaper).

By and large, the media, the Directorate of Health and researchers all have the same attitude: in 2020, movement equals exercise.

Another reason why we tend not to think of work in relation to exercise is that we often perceive physical effort in the workplace as detrimental. As the Directorate points out, there was a time when our daily lives involved more physical activity than was good for our bodies. But does that necessarily mean that physical work is undesirable in and of itself?

According to Stein Knardal, a researcher at the National Institute of Occupational Health in Norway (STAMI), the pain that we experience as either unproblematic or positive in connection with exercise is, in fact, the very same pain that we deem to be bad for us in a work context.

We know that physical exercise is good for us, so there is every likelihood that training has a placebo effect. And the more expensive the placebo, the greater the effect, Knardal says. In other words, an expensive gym works wonders for back pain.

But what about the opposite of a placebo – a nocebo? A nocebo is an imagined negative effect that results from negative expectations. The best known examples tend to be the side effects of medicine. But could the pain caused by physical work also be a nocebo?

We have, for example, been taught to avoid heavy lifting. Especially repeated heavy lifting. It's not good for our backs. Yet research has not found any strong link between heavy lifting and back pain. On the other hand, research *does* show that employees who are not happy at work often have more physical complaints than those who are.[17]

Variety makes you strong

I don't, by any means, wish to deny that heavy, monotonous work is not good for your body. We are, after all, generalists, even when we're at work: we're designed to do a little of everything. Perhaps that is the key.

Because just think what we are capable of when the circumstances are right. I'm talking about those of us who are not necessarily elite athletes, but who move because the consequences of our movements are important to us. How much heavy work can our bodies tolerate, and how hard should we work them? How much truth is there in the old adage 'a change is as good as a rest'? How much can we achieve? How can we prevent hard work from making us ill, and instead find pleasure in the effort?

There is one person I want to ask, someone I have long seen as a role model: small-scale farmer Bente Getz from Guleiksgarden, her farm in Samnanger in Midhordaland.

Bente makes the only *gamalost* that I like. It might be called *gamalost*, which means 'old cheese', but it's actually fresh, just mould-ripened.

She was also one of the first people in Norway to make cheese from sheep's milk. Bente keeps dairy cows and dairy sheep, is a cheesemaker and baker, provides tourist accommodation, runs direct sales, has a vegetable and herb garden, and peacocks – and she achieves all this in summer, because in winter the road to her farm is closed.

Bente doesn't invest vast sums of money in big, expensive buildings and even more expensive loans. But she does invest in herself. And in her family farm and everything that she can get out of it. She invests her body, motivation, courage and willingness to learn. Which means long, long working days. Is that really possible without wearing yourself out?

I set myself the task of shadowing Bente one fine summer's day. We meet in the bakery at five o'clock in the morning.

The dough we prepared the evening before has to be baked, rolls have to be rolled and cheesecake has to be made. Bente uses her own farm milk for the rolls and her own cheese for the cheesecake and pizza pinwheels. On weekdays, she sells her delicious wares at LAGA, a cooperative set up by local small-scale producers in the community centre. At the weekend, she sells her bread, cakes, mature cheese and cured meats, among other things, at markets and festivals.

Bente has learned to make all these things relatively late in life, which is one of the reasons I admire her so much: because she dares. It would have been hard to predict that she would one day become a smallholder. Her first career was with IBM, where she helped to develop the marketing department, and was once put up in one of Oslo's fanciest hotels for three months. But it became monotonous in the end. Bente wanted to get out and see the world. So she did just that, living in various different places before finally settling in Israel with her husband and children.

Until it was time to come home. To Guleiks-garden, which had been unoccupied for more than fifty years since her grandparents moved away. The land was rented out, but Bente felt the pull of her roots. She wanted to get the land back. And to do that, she needed to use her body.

It's just gone six o'clock, and we are on our way to the milking shed. Four cows and six dairy sheep are housed here. Bente uses a milking machine for the cows, but does the sheep by hand. Fodder has to be carried in and muck has to be shovelled out. These animals are essential to her income and life on the farm, and it's not hard to see how much they mean to her. The byre has been modernised only as much as is necessary – that's to say, not much. The cows are small Jerseys that fit neatly into the old stalls. And as long as the weather and ground permit, they're let out to play every day.

'The locals laughed at me when I said I was going to live off four cows and six sheep. But not many of them are laughing now. I don't have much, but I make the most of what I've got,' Bente tells me, from behind a cow.

However, part of the job is also to recognise that she can't do everything herself. She gets help with the most difficult part – the accounts. The second-toughest job is harvesting fodder. She now buys all her coarse feed from her neighbours, which frees all her land for grazing.

'The rest I can manage alone, as long as I keep healthy,' she says.

After attending to the animals, it's back to the bakery for the last round of baking. The milk from the byre has to be used while it's fresh, and is transformed into cheese for future cheesecakes.

Next we have a good breakfast, packed with calories. After all, we've been up for a good four hours now. And after breakfast, it's time to pack all our wares into the car and drive down to the shop. We chat on the way.

'I didn't know much when I started, but I've never been afraid of trying something new. And I'm not afraid to call it a day, either. If it hadn't worked, I would have stopped,' Bente says.

The afternoon is spent doing whatever is most needed. That might be gathering herbs to dry, repairing a fence, harvesting vegetables, tidying the barn, scratching the peacock behind the ear, welcoming guests, or anything else that might crop up. In any case, it is soon time to go back to the bakery. The dough for the next day has to be prepared before the evening chores in the byre. The cows are already waiting by the gate. The evening passes and, by nine o'clock, we're ready for the last ritual of the day: dinner and a glass of good wine.

'Of course it's hard work. Physically demanding.

The long workdays in summer do nothing for my arthritis. But I manage, because the work is varied and I don't do the same thing all day long,' Bente says. She's tired, but relaxed and happy.

She's always glad when winter comes, leaving her snowed in with the television and a clear conscience. She uses those four or five months of the year to recharge and build her energy and strength.

Having said that, Bente is a dynamo. Not everyone could live the way she does. All too few can muster her confidence that everything will be all right. But without even trying, she's an inspiration – it's effortless. Well, almost.

Was everything better in the good old days?

My newly wattled juniper wall is green and beautiful on the outside, but it's also thick and bushy. The foliage sticks well out from the wall and of course looks totally disproportionate on a wall as small as this one, rather than a large barn wall. But it will shrink over time as it dries out. According to the book, the greenery will turn orange, then grey, after which a layer of moss will grow over it all, and hold it in place.

The big surprise comes when I look inside. I haven't given the inside wall much thought, to be honest – I've never really considered the toilet as a place you'd sit for a long time, admiring your surroundings. Until now.

Because, wow, seeing how the branches weave in and out of each other on the inside is beautiful. The battens and foliage are hidden on the inside, only the branches are visible. It's a bit like sitting in a basket. I want the wall to be ready. Fast.

Because, yes, I find the slowness of the work challenging. It's like there are two people with conflicting interests. There's the one who gathers the juniper branches and wants to get back to the wall as quickly as possible. It's all too easy for her to think, 'OK, this bit isn't perfect, but it'll do somewhere,' and collect and take back branches that have too little foliage, or are too stiff, or have too many twigs, just because they are there in front of her, and it won't take so long to fill the rope. This, of course, annoys the other one who, a few minutes later, is working on the wall and picks up branch after branch that is unusable, unless she takes the time and effort to modify them so they can be woven into place.

They may not always agree, but they are both intent on the same thing: getting the wall finished. One more branch. One more batten. Out to the bushes – one more load of branches. Weaving. I reach a corner at the end of one wall. It takes time. But things speed up. Suddenly I'm over halfway. No more branches. Load up again. It starts raining. It stops raining. The news on the radio – hours must have passed. I take a break. Check the time and leap back into action – there must have been several news reports since I last listened.

As I trot back to the cabin to pack my bags, I realise that I haven't checked my emails since yesterday. That doesn't happen often, certainly not this late in the day. Not even my normally powerful Facebook addiction has encroached on my desire to push on with the most beautiful wall I have ever made. But I won't get it finished in a day. Reality comes knocking: society operates in such a way that I won't be paid for my work on the wall, so I have to earn my keep by other means.

Though you might not believe it from my

Instagram feed, I am primarily a writer, speaker and social commentator. I make a living from writing opinion pieces, columns, articles and books, and talking to others. I write about where our food comes from, about the primary sector, coastal culture, the power of the major food retailers, and I comment on current affairs. I enjoy my work: it's important and exciting. And I like being part of the public debate, having a voice.

But as chopping wood and weaving juniper make for much better photo ops than sitting in front of a tired old Mac, these are the ones I post in the world of shared images. As a result, on the rare occasions that I do meet any of my followers, they always say: 'So you've moved to a cabin in the forest then?'

The fact is that I haven't, much as I'd like to. At the end of the day, I'm happy to have a home with running water and electricity. I love watching TV series and the news at nine.

I need both the outdoorsy, simple life and the modern conveniences. And I'm quite good at living within my means. I'm not too worried if the hours I work don't give me what amounts to a full-time salary every month – some months, like this one, they give me more and at other times a good deal less. And I use my spare time to look after the part of me that doesn't get used when I'm writing. It's good for both me and my work. I don't feel even a smidgen of guilt when I spend a Wednesday morning picking mushrooms, butchering a lamb that I've bought from a farmer I know, or chopping down spruce trees at the cabin. We have to allow ourselves a little luxury, and these are mine – considerably greener than city breaks in Prague and the latest must-have gadget. Or at least I think so.

That's why I will ignore my emails and return to my privy wall, even if it doesn't earn me a penny. It will be finished and it will work, because juniper branches are no different today from how they were when juniper cladding was more common.

Halfway up a mountain, far from people, power lines and concrete-and-steel council offices with bookshelves full of multiple editions of the planning regulations, I have found a useful resource. Quite possibly the perfect resource for my purposes. And believe me, I've learned a thing or two about juniper in the process. Not least, that even though it grows in abundance, it's actually sometimes possible to have too little of it.

I don't expect anyone to pay me for what I've discovered, or for the work I've done on my wall. But I do think society should embrace such discoveries, resources and work, without irony, without romantic nostalgia, simply because, in this situation, it is the best practical solution. And because, as far as I can see, it does no one any harm and it does me a lot of good.

It frustrates me that I can't say that the experience I gain is as valuable as the money I'm paid for overtime without undermining my position by appearing eccentric. Because I think a lot of people would agree. I think many of us have something old in our lives that we want to preserve, techniques we want to master, walls we want to build.

Might we not do well to set aside our fear of nostalgia for a moment and consider what the generations before us have achieved? Think about those huge juniper-wattle walls on barns made from timber that had been felled and cut with an axe and saw, then laid on top of a dry-stone wall. The very same hands that made those walls then mended the holes in a pair of trousers, cut the grass with a scythe and wove baskets that were used to carry manure from the dunghill. Just think of all the things we could do back then.

More often than not, when I express something like that, I'm told not to be nostalgic. Not to romanticise the toil, not to fall into the trap of thinking that everything was better in the good old days – not an ideal position when you want to be taken seriously in public debate. To a certain extent, I understand: the past is the past, we've moved on, nothing can ever be copied, and believing that we solve a problem by turning back the clock is naive, at best.

Yet, while things may not have *been* better, the majority of people *were a lot better at* a number of things than we are now. And some of those things are still needed. So why should we be afraid to talk about it?

I see heroes of old everywhere. I don't know their names, but they're there and they have often just become part of the landscape. The first time I became aware of them was in the mountains between Aurland, in Sogn og Fjordane, and

Hallingdal. One morning, they were suddenly everywhere I looked: the old drovers' paths, a milkshed, a tree that bears the traces of once being harvested for feed. In all of them, I saw old sweat, old toil, old labour and old, dilapidated pride.

Beneath my feet, the main road between Hol and Aurland thundered through a tunnel; bus drivers and car drivers and motorcyclists all complained about the narrow lanes, oncoming traffic and lack of light in the tunnel. And in front of me was a steep path. Up the mountain on one side, straight down to Låvisberget and Vassbygdvatnet 700 metres below on the other, twisting and turning and devoid of a white middle line. No one would think of this path, which is also a road of sorts, in any context other than hiking. Not even me. The fact that it is steep and a hard climb is part of the fun, and what makes it so memorable – and it keeps you fit.

But this particular path is more than that. As I walked that morning, it struck me that this used to be the main road. Once upon a time, the path over Grindsfjellet was one of the main routes between eastern and western Norway.

Today, the area is best known as a place for

family hikes. Aurlandsdalen, the eighth most popular walking route in Norway, is only a few kilometres northeast of where I'm standing. I can see down into the valley from here. Aurlandsdalen Lodge at Østerbø is a favourite starting point, and every year, hundreds of hikers set off down the valley from here. Some may know that it is one of the oldest paths in the country, dating all the way back to the seventeenth century; for many, one of the main reasons for choosing this particular hike is its cultural history (as well as the fact that it is largely downhill). It passes the old farms of Viki and Nesbø, and you can catch a glimpse of Berekvam and Teigen farms too, through the scrubby trees, before taking a welcome break at the majestic Sinjarheim farm.

These days, it is almost overgrown with trees and undergrowth, which are of no use to anyone. But in the 1800s, this was the heart of the community, whereas Vangen, which is now the administrative centre, was no more than a cluster of turf-roofed houses around the church. The most valuable resources were in the mountains: rough grazing land where livestock and reindeer could find food.

*

In 1835, the population of Aurlandsdalen was at its peak. One hundred and three people lived in the valley which was so steep and narrow that you couldn't even make a path without adding ladders here and there. In 1846, the 11 farms kept 146 cattle and 157 sheep, as well as draught horses.[18]

It's hard to imagine how much effort this took. When the farms were in operation, there was a huge demand for the grazing grounds that are now overgrown and closing in from all sides. The pastures were – and still are – some of the best in the whole of Vestlandet. Having spent the whole summer up here grazing, every autumn, around 15,000 to 20,000 cattle came down from the mountains. The herdsmen drove more than 1,000 cattle over the mountains to the markets in eastern Norway.

If you go into the main house at Sinjarheim, you will see a picture that gives some idea of the strength that was needed. There is a photograph of the last working horse on the farm. She was a Fjord horse and was small, even for the breed, but no less strong for it. The difference between this Fjord horse and the average horse found on farms and in riding stables today is roughly equivalent to the difference between Usain Bolt and Justin Bieber: the Sinjarheim horse looks like she had an extra layer of muscle.

In 1866, they farmed nearly 3 acres of cereal and potatoes at Sinjarheim, which is more cereal than was grown and harvested in the entire municipality of Sogn og Fjordane in 2018.[19]

But to go back to my point: we should be wary of romanticising. Hard physical work is not so much fun when it's all you do from dawn until dusk, from childhood to old age. It is said that one of the last people to live at Sinjarheim only remembers being allowed to play once as a child. And local historian Anders Onstad tells the following anecdote from the farm at Berekvam: 'There was one winter when they weren't able to keep the main house warm. So they moved out into the byre and down into the cellar, wherever there were animals to keep them warm. They even spent Christmas there.'

Vast numbers of people emigrated to escape this life, mostly to America. And can you blame them? But equally, many of them then longed to come home.

Very few people from 2020 would have the stamina to live a 1920s existence, and no doubt only a handful of people from the 1920s would turn down today's lifestyle if offered the choice. Fortunately, we don't have to choose. We can take the best of both worlds.

If nothing else, the environment would benefit from us not losing the ability to use the resources around us. An argument that is rarely heard in the current climate debate. Where is the desire to make the best possible use of what we already have instead of constantly looking for something more, be that technology, higher productivity or greater efficiency?

Why don't we pick our apples from the tree in the garden instead of buying them in the shop? Why don't we repair the zip on a jacket instead of buying a new one? Because we have too much money? Because we don't need to any longer, or because we no longer see the value in being thrifty and careful? Maybe we no longer even know how to be thrifty and careful.

'Robust' is currently a buzzword in the public sector and government policy. One reform after another has been introduced to help us build a 'more robust society', and I can only agree it would be a good thing. But instead of building a solid structure – after all, that is what robust means, a structure that is literally or metaphorically capable of withstanding all kinds of threats and dangers – by merging government bodies, municipalities and offices, I think we should build a more robust society by ensuring that more of us have access to the knowledge on which society is built. Would we not, for example, be less exposed to danger if more of us knew how the electrics in a house work? If more of us knew how to milk a cow, grow potatoes, change a tyre, tie a secure knot in a piece of rope in order to save someone who needs it?

Not so that we can set up in competition with electricians, farmers or rescue teams, but rather because these skills afford both individuals and society greater safety. Spreading knowledge creates a more solid base – a more robust foundation for society, as I see it. That's certainly how I feel: the more general and practical understanding I have, the safer I feel and the more daring I become.

For example, assuming responsibility for the life

and adventures of 168 goats may sound daunting at first, but given the right knowledge and enough practice, it can be an amazing experience.

Goat summer

The reason that I walked those magical paths in Aurlandsdalen was that I had taken on a job that is almost extinct. I was a dairymaid, a goat maid to be precise, and was responsible for 131 goats and 37 kids. Every morning at dawn, they stood ready for me and every evening at five they were waiting outside the goat shed in Stondalen (a valley off Aurlandsdalen), 620 metres above sea level.

There, the day starts at six o'clock. As soon as the goats see my head pop round the barn door, they jump to their feet. Grey, white, pied and blue. Long and thin, or more rotund, all 131 goats can feel in their udders it's time to be milked, and all 168, including the kids, know that it's time for food and a cuddle. 'Good morning, gang,' I say. 'Maaa,' they say. I switch on the milking machine. This is how I would like every day to start.

There's room for twenty-four goats in the

milking parlour. I have twelve clusters with two milking cups apiece. Two tubes run from each cup: one that sends the pulse signal and another that carries the milk. The pulsators are controlled by a pump that steadily draws the milk from both udders – one is pumped while the other rests.

I'm not always fully awake, so I take a thermo-cup of coffee with me from the house, but I never fill it more than half full. Because this is where I cut out the middleman, topping up straight from the source. The second goat from the right has large, fine teats and gives milk easily. I close my right hand around the right teat and, finger by finger, squeeze a jet of milk straight into the cup. After about eight or ten squeezes, I have enough frothy milk for the world's freshest caffè latte.

The work is repetitive: on with the milking cup, off with the milking cup, out with the goats that have been milked, in with the next lot. And all the while, the pump pulses over my head: 'Ta-tikk, ta-takk, ta-tikk, ta-takk.' At half-past six in the morning, it could send you back to sleep, but I actually find it gives me rhythm. A working rhythm. Flow. That essential feeling that is actually a non-feeling, because when it's there, you don't notice, it happens without thinking: the jobs just get done, hands and head and body work together, do, carry on, know, understand – until, suddenly, all 131 goats have been milked and I stand there not knowing quite how I did it, but I did, and I'm confident that I did it well, because this is something I can do.

I said the job is 'almost extinct' because only 1 per cent of all the *støl* – mountain summer farms, or shielings – that existed in Norway after the war are currently still in use. So you could say that the green lifestyle is nothing new, it was something we already had many decades ago – but then switched from green to brown and grey.

The idea of making the switch back to green seems popular. All the political parties and nine out of ten Norwegians would like to see more Norwegian food produced from Norway's green resources. And those we have most of are grass and mountains. Norway's largest producer of dairy products, TINE, sells *Sætersmør* – mountain butter – which has never been anywhere near a mountain flower, because it knows the name appeals. The meat from animals that graze in the mountains is healthier and of better quality than that from animals which are kept in barns and given fodder that has been transported halfway across the globe.

So we have both the desire and good reason to bring animals back to our mountains and to invest the old paths with purpose again. We also have technology that previous generations could only have dreamed of. We can now get to the shieling in Stondalen not by foot but by car – with trailers. We no longer need to spend half a day standing around stirring our traditional brown goat's cheese in an iron pot, unless we really want to; instead we put the milk straight into a temperature-controlled milk tank that TINE then comes and empties two or three times a week. We can put GPS collars on our animals to help us find them, should they get lost or stuck in a crevice, and we can send out helicopters or drones to locate our sheep in autumn, and use taxpayers' money to subsidise farmers to look after nature for us.

But none of these modern conveniences mean that I'm any less proud of the work that I do in the byre.

There are still things that have to be done by hand. Even though I have a milking machine, which means that I can milk twelve goats at the same time, I have to make sure that each teat is milked properly, that the udder is emptied, but not milked dry. If I take too little, our profits will be down and there's a risk of engorgement, and if I take too much, the goat might get an udder infection. Some teats fit the milking cups better than others, and the ones that don't fit as well need a little help: I have to lift a little, pull a little. After a while, my hands learn how much pressure is needed in the cup and the teat for them to work well together.

Whenever I have visitors, I realise that I now treat the udders, teats, individual goats and flock as a whole very differently from a novice. That may, of course, seem obvious, but I haven't noticed the changes happening. Goats have a lot of personality, and if you manage to work with them, rather than against them, you'll make things a whole lot easier for yourself. You have to be firm, have a plan, know where they are going and how they are going to get there. And make time for a cuddle. Or two. Or lots.

Goats like to be scratched behind the ear as well, preferably while they nuzzle my face or try to pull off my scarf. They smell good, sweet and goaty, warmed by the sun and fresh from the pasture. It's impossible to be sad when you know you can snuggle up to a warm goat.

The work is meaningful. It is here, as a dairymaid, surrounded by the goats and the mountains, that I feel I am of most value to myself and the rest of the world.

However, it seems that the rest of the world does not entirely agree. As a seasonal worker, my hourly pay is 124.15 Norwegian kroner, which gives me a monthly wage of around 19,000 kroner. In other words, 41 per cent of the average wage in Norway[20] and 4,000 kroner less than what I earned as a part-time editor for the weekly newspaper *Dag og Tid* in 2015.

The disparate and distorted value of work in hard cash terms. Fortunately, I only need to look out of the dairy shed door for an alternative measure of value, as I see how important the goats are for the ecosystem. A river and an upland fence run the length of Stondalen. On the side where my goats are, the vegetation is lush, low and varied. There is no grazing on the other side and the mountain birch and willow grow so close that they're almost impassable.

Why is it that we're unable to use more than half of the grazing land we have in our mountains? Overgrowth, as it's called, is a problem not only in terms of blocking the way for hikers, but also for food production and the ecosystem and biological diversity.

But could this not also be a rallying cry to use our hands? This is a question that has not been widely discussed. Even though Norwegian nature looks untouched, it seldom is. Only 12 per cent of Norway is classified as wilderness. A further 44 per cent of our country is defined as being 'without major infrastructure development', but that does not mean that we humans have not had a hand in shaping the landscape.

We tend to think that the agrarian landscape is important for tourism in general, but surveys of both foreign and Norwegian tourists have shown that this cultivated landscape is in fact most important to us Norwegians.[21]

And is that not even more reason to look after

145

it? It's not just the result – the view, the landscape itself – that matters, but also the fact that we are no longer able to sustain a lifestyle that is part of who we are. Most of us can't rebuild the dry-stone walls that are falling down, nor can we mow the small strips of hayfield around the shielings; we don't know how to harvest leaves and prune branches from the avenues of pollarded trees that line the cultivated grazing land. We are in danger of losing these crafts, traditions and skills. Buried beneath the overgrowth is layer upon layer of lost mastery and satisfaction.

And it is precisely this sense of mastery and satisfaction that I experience with my juniper branches. I could also boldly claim that my small juniper-wattling project is helping to clear the agrarian landscape as well. A reasonable amount of juniper bushes is good. Too much juniper not only hinders walkers and grazing, but also blocks the view. Juniper is one of the species responsible for overgrowth in the landscape. The gathering and use of juniper therefore benefits both me and the landscape.

And it is this symbiosis, the fact that we can

create something together and benefit each other, that is the greatest joy of all. Walking along a path when you understand it gives a different pleasure from simply seeing it and walking along it. When I use the landscape around me, I become a part of it in a completely different way than when I pass through it. Society may not put a price on it, but surely this is what's truly valuable.

FIVE

*In which I teach myself something
that's almost too niche for YouTube*

Hands can grip, weigh, discern, interpret and understand. They can lift, position, reach out and save whatever is about to fall down, stick a thread straight through the eye of a needle and then press it through the wrinkled fabric in stitches that are even on the back as well, where it's not visible to the eye. Hands are firm and steady when they know what they are doing, and can feel their way gingerly through a room when it's too dark for our eyes. They stretch out boldly into the unknown.

Sometimes they gently wipe away tears from another person's face. But never forget that they can strike within a nanosecond, if needs be. Put a violin in the right hands, and they can conjure up universal emotions in thousands of people in a great concert hall. They can cross fingers, touch wood, throw salt over a shoulder and stop a black cat from crossing your path by picking it up, holding it in the crook of your arm and making it purr with pleasure.

And once upon a time, you may have sat at a table with way too many fingers of your own and not been able to find anything to talk about because you were so conscious of your fingers that wouldn't stop fidgeting – until they found another set of fingers, which were equally confused and frustrated, on the other side of the table and all twenty of them realised that this was where they belonged.

Yes, I think about hands a lot. My own as well. All that they can and can't do. Sometimes, when I sit down at a piano, I'm overcome with wonder and admiration: how can they remember that Debussy piece that I haven't played for around five years, or is it six? Because it has to be my hands that remember – my head rarely has a clue, certainly not about details. How do they give expression to the music?

At other times, they can't even thud their way through something as basic as 'Bella Ciao' on the accordion. My stupid fingers make mistakes and don't seem to work together at all.

'It's important to you to have hard skin on your hands, isn't it?' my mother remarked in passing recently, and I realised she was right. In the same way that I feel sexier, stronger, more feminine and confident when I wear work clothes – a baseball cap, dungarees and a vest that shows off my shoulder muscles, because all this physical work means they've become quite defined – than I do in a dress, tights and lipstick, I'm happiest when I'm using my hands. I most often feel like showing off my hands when there's a good, hard callus on the lower joint of my fingers, when the nails and cuticles are dirty and there's the odd splinter or small cut that I've covered with gaffer tape (the wound doesn't hurt, doesn't need a plaster, but it's a bit inconvenient when it bleeds everywhere).

When my hands start to itch, I know that they're telling me I've been working at the computer for too long, that the good, coarse skin on my hands from manual work is thinning, and if I don't do something, my hands will once again be smooth and soft within days. It happens so fast – in the course of a week, all the good work has disappeared.

*

The truth is that how I feel about myself is to a great extent determined by what my hands can do. It goes both ways. And right now, as I stand in a car park somewhere outside Rælingen, I feel very small and alone. The feeling's crept up on me from behind. I'm staying in Oslo, and have had to take two buses to get here. And now I stand staring at the shop door, wondering whether I'm brave enough to go in.

The shop almost certainly has a tool that I want to try with my own two hands: a froe. I want to test my practical understanding.

A froe is, in reality, a combined knife and axe. It has a narrow, rectangular blade with a 30-centimetre edge. The edge is convex, like that of an axe, but it's designed to cut or wedge, not to chop. The haft sits loosely in an eyelet in the blade, at a right angle.

It may not look like a very useful tool, as it's both heavy and unbalanced, but a froe is exactly what I need if I – perhaps as the first person in history – am going to try to make shingles from Sitka spruce.

Most of the walls of my privy are now covered in juniper wattle. Half of the back wall is finished with a removable steel plate, in case the waste needs to be removed. So I have one and a bit walls left, one of which has the door in it, which means it is small and narrow, making it tricky to clad with juniper. I also think it would look rather odd.

And anyway, the snow came early this year. Suddenly my juniper branches were buried and inaccessible. So I started to think about what else I could do with my final wall. And I remembered wood shingles. Jon Godal mentioned them in his book and I realised that I'd also seen them on stave church roofs: thin, flat roof 'tiles' of wood, cut, hewn or carved from logs cut to the right length, along the grain so the growth rings are maintained, and then placed at least halfway over each other in several rows. When correctly laid, they are snug enough to prevent water getting in.

The shingles can be planed, fitted and tarred or oiled, so that they protect against water, rot and damp for as long as any other roofing material. Shingle roofs have been found that date from the thirteenth century, which means they have lasted for over eight hundred years.

It goes without saying that my shingles will

not be so meticulously made. They won't last as long either, even though they are going to be on a vertical wall rather than laid on a roof, and will therefore be less exposed to damp. But Sitka spruce is not the ideal quality for roof shingles: the growth rings on old shingles are no more than 2 millimetres wide, and the shingles are free of knots. The growth rings in my trees are between 8 and 10 millimetres and the wood is by no means knot free. But still, I'd like to give it a try. Do I dare go into the shop and tell them this? Do I dare go into the shop at all?

Yes, you could say that I have a fear of specialist shops. Shops that are full of people who are more knowledgeable than me. I know that's precisely why the shop exists: to help me make the right choices, so that I can learn more and buy the right things. But I still don't like being here, in the same way that I don't like taking the car to the garage to get the brakes fixed or calling a plumber, or going to the hairdresser, for that matter. Strange, I know.

I muster my courage – I've come this far, I can't just turn around again – and I go into the shop. I see a froe straight away and, in the same moment, I hear that dreaded question: 'How can I help you?'

So I jump right in: I tell him about the cabin and the privy and my unsuitable Sitka spruce. The shop assistant understands immediately: 'Ah, it's a froe you need, then.'

'Is it difficult to use?' I ask – I might as well, while I'm at it.

'Well, is there any skill that's easy?'

The shop assistant gives me a wry look. I sigh, smile, pay and leave – one froe richer. And that feels good.

So now I just need to do all the rest – like work out how to use it. As far as I am aware, no one I know has ever used a froe. And I can't find any good videos in Norwegian on YouTube – which is a clear indication that whatever it is you're doing is pretty niche. According to Godal, however, it's not particularly difficult – a skilled craftsman can make up to 1,000 shingles a day. So I just have to give it a go.

I have some fresh logs ready. I cut them into 33-centimetre lengths (because I've read that this is how long shingles should be when they are for a wall), and I do a relatively good job of avoiding the worst twigs and branches. Then I put the haft into the eyelet in the blade. It feels far too loose. I knock it in a couple of times with a sledge-hammer. Is it secure now?

I place the blade across a log that is about 20 centimetres in diameter. Hold the haft steady in my left hand, and use my right to hit the blade with the sledge-hammer – and absolutely nothing happens. The blade shows no sign of even biting into the wood. I try again. And again. Then the haft loosens and shoots up out of the eyelet, and my hand, which was gripping it, follows. It hurts. Damn! The haft flies through the air – I appear to have thrown it.

And so I carry on for some time. Banging, hitting, trying, achieving nothing. Apart from getting more and more hot and bothered. The haft keeps coming loose and I cannot get the blade to bite. I take a deep breath and get a bucket of water. Put the wooden haft in the water, and then go for a long stomp, uphill.

The next morning, I leave the haft where it is. Instead, I get out my biggest splitting axe and a piece of wood. I position the axe in the middle of the log and hit it with the piece of wood (I wouldn't dare believe that I could be so precise just hitting it with the axe), and cleave the log with two blows. I do the same thing again – cleave the halves in two – not a problem.

But I have to try the froe again. I lift the haft out of the bucket; it has definitely swelled and sits more securely in the blade – which bodes well. I position the blade about a centimetre in from the edge of the quarter log, so it cuts from the centre out. There is a good deal of room on either side of the blade. I carefully hit the end of the blade as I hold on to the haft with all my might – and hallelujah, it works. The knife cuts into the wood, mainly on the outer edge, so I have to hit the blade again between the haft and the log, and again, it works. By now, though, the shingle is getting a little too thin; the knife digs deeper out towards the edge so I carry on banging as I try to straighten it. But that doesn't work: about halfway down, the knife pops out. But even if it's only half as long as it should be, I have my first shingle.

And I get better at it. On the next attempt, I manage to cleave the log the whole way and produce a good, flat shingle which is 33 centimetres long, 20 to 25 centimetres wide and about a centimetre thick. I put it to one side and make another. And a third. Soon I have a pile.

Every now and then I hit a knot. I knock my way through. Sometimes the shingle splinters. Then it becomes firewood, kindling, which is always useful. When the log becomes too narrow for shingles, it's consigned to the wood pile. I chop it with the axe. Done. Gradually I learn to feel with my haft hand where the blade is going and can adjust it by adding weight and altering where I hit with the sledge-hammer. It's fun.

And it feels great to get the shingles up on the wall too. The first thing I realise is that I can't secure the nails into thin air. So I try to put up some horizontal poles, but the battens that I have to hand are not strong enough, and they break, offering no resistance to the hammer and nail.

Once again, I'm grateful that I have an almost endless supply of timber, as I end up laying logs horizontally to create the wall, and then nailing the shingles to the logs. I tap a small nail through the first shingle, then I place the next one on top with an overlap. A nail through the overlap then holds the first and the second shingle in place. More fun.

It's quick work. My hands are happy playing with the hammer and nails, they like it, can't move on to the next one fast enough. Up and up until I have to get out the ladder. My body feels light. I take the time to have a coffee break up there, lean my head back and look up at the tree tops, think to myself that they're not so bad after all, my Sitka spruces.

My trees don't grow straight up: they twist around themselves, as trees often do when they grow too fast or are surrounded by too many other trees. As a result, not all of my shingles are flat, and some have knots in them – in other words, my wall is not entirely flush. But so be it. If they fall off, I can always make new ones. In fact, I almost hope that some shingles do fall off so that I can make more.

The outside edge of the nail on my left pinkie is purple. My right hand is still vibrating from all the blows with the sledge-hammer. I have an irritating blister on the palm between my ring finger and little finger. The skin around my nails is torn and I need to put on some cream, and I have to remember to get all the splinters out of my left thumb. Why can't every day be like this?

The heritage you touch rather than see

At the end of the day, I hang the hammer up in the lean-to outside the cabin. What would I have done without it? The hammer has been a useful tool all day, but it is also a symbol of ability. The ability to hit a nail straight in, preferably with one hand because the other is holding the plank. In many ways, it's the very definition of craftsmanship. 'He can't even hit a nail,' we say, even though hitting a nail is far from easy, especially if it's going to be done properly, so that you're able to hammer nails in all day without getting tendonitis, or having a constantly bruised thumb; and especially if you can't stand upright and hammer straight ahead, which is almost always the case. If the area where you're hammering in the nail will be visible afterwards, you certainly can't afford to miss, because then the hammer marks will show.

But it is possible to learn to hit the nail. We can all learn, by doing it over and over and over again, with a little correction along the way. Or we can learn from someone else. It's a tradition that should be continually passed on.

Yes, I have made a wall, but I've done it in a way

that many others have before me. And as I don't need to reinvent the wheel, there's a kind of quality assurance to the technique. One might even go as far as to call it cultural heritage. Although my wall may never be worthy of a preservation order, I am a bearer of intangible cultural heritage – a concept that places as much importance on preserving the process as the end product.

And this principle of intangible cultural heritage is why it is so important that we continue to make *bunad* – traditional Norwegian costumes – ourselves, even if they can be and are made cheaper in China. We cannot abandon Norwegian farming and let the Danes produce our brown cheese for us, because then we'll forget how it's made. We can't leave all woodcarving to computer-programmed machines or catch all our fish with echo-sounders.

Immaterial cultural heritage is a relatively new concept, first established in UNESCO's *Convention for the Safeguarding of the Intangible Cultural Heritage* in 2003. The concept was defined here to include the practices, representations, expressions, knowledge and skills that a society recognises as part of its cultural heritage. Cultural expressions are those that have been passed from generation to generation, in interaction with nature and history, and still generate a feeling of identity and continuity.[22]

It sounds great, doesn't it, even in these abstract terms? I like the idea that I can interact with nature and history to create an identity by doing something concrete. And better yet, the convention states that one person's culture in no way prevents others from having their own. On the contrary, it's easier to accept other cultural expressions when we are aware of our own.

Norway ratified the convention in 2007 and Arts Council Norway was given responsibility for its implementation. But the convention hasn't received much attention, and far fewer people have heard about intangible cultural heritage than the World Heritage Sites, even though they are two sides of the same coin. Norway has eight World Heritage Sites, but only two cultural expressions on the list of intangible cultural heritage: the traditional music and dance in Setesdal, and the Oselvar boat-building technique.

*

At the time that the convention was ratified, five voluntary folk and craft organisations were appointed as ambassadors for intangible cultural heritage in Norway.[23] This was a smart move: it should not be left to museums to take care of our intangible cultural heritage. It has to be kept alive in society, so community groups and individuals are important. Even though 'cultural heritage' is a rather grand expression, it rarely involves any pomp.

The Netherlands, for example, has included the craft of the miller operating traditional windmills and watermills on their list of representative intangible practices. Germany has registered the art of building and playing the organ; Peru has registered a traditional system of water distribution in the agricultural district of Corongo under the authority of a community 'water judge', who is also responsible for the organisation of festivals; Belgium has registered its beer culture, and France the gastronomic meal that starts with an aperitif, has at least four successive courses and finishes with more alcohol.

It is things like this that make the world more diverse and everyday life more enjoyable. We could live without each individual element, but when you look at the bigger picture, it is precisely these small details that make it vibrant and exciting.

Finding culture in shawls and soup

The Norwegian Folk Art and Craft Association is the organisation that has done most to systematise intangible cultural heritage in Norway. They have an ongoing project where they let local associations draw up red lists of local crafts and techniques that are in danger of being lost. However, unlike red lists of flora and fauna, they go beyond simply identifying what is at risk.

Whenever a local branch of the association identifies such a craft, they then also learn it. All around the country, old skills such as wool-dyeing with plants and making wooden beer casks have been relayed to new heads and hands.

One project in particular stands out: the Folgefonn branch and the making of the Hardanger *bunad* headpiece. In 2016, when the association teamed up with the local museum to start the project, there was only one woman left who practised the intricate technique. One in the whole world.

The Hardanger *bunad* headpiece, which is made of either linen or cotton, is supposed to 'sweep over the head like the Folgefonna glacier over the mountain'. In order to achieve this effect, the material has to be starched and folded in an intricate pattern. A headpiece for special occasions can have up to 300 folds. Since the project started, they have held multiple courses, and even though no one has yet taken it up professionally, the craft is now far from forgotten.

Many of the crafts on the red list use common-place materials – which are increasingly removed from our daily lives. And the less we know about local techniques, the more likely we are to dismiss as waste what was previously seen as a commodity. If you only know how, soft rushes can be used to make shoes, nettles can be transformed into fabric, the hairs from a cow's tail can become insulating insoles, and birch bark can be used for so much more than turf roofs and kindling – how about a lunchbox, or a wallet, or a rucksack?

Yes, it all sounds like rather hard work, worthy

and old-fashioned. But nothing could be more local and environmentally friendly than products made from things that you have around you or could source locally – if the system was made to source that way, rather than buying most things from China. Is that not resource efficiency?

Perhaps the greatest threat to our cultural heritage is a distorted interpretation of the word 'efficiency'. As soon as we take it to mean faster, simpler and cheaper, then traditional methods lose out.

I am more interested than most in food and food production, but for a long time I was unable to explain why this subject fascinated me so much. Then one day, I stumbled over the answer in an American blog: 'I like making food and I love eating – but intellectually, I am drawn to food because it links human culture with nature and the environment.'[24]

Our natural environment determines what food we can produce, and we in turn shape our natural environment producing this food. And I believe that as many of us as possible should be directly involved in this process.

The kitchen is another place where I rely on

my hands. Even though my ability to cut meat is far from that of a professional butcher, I'm not fazed when half a lamb lands on the kitchen table each autumn. I know where the shoulder is, how to separate the leg and shank, and how far back the loin goes. Through years of practice, my hands can guide the knife so the different cuts are good enough for my use.

I know how to make plum jam and put it into sterilised jars that can be stored in the outhouse for months. And I can look after a sourdough and bake a moist, light brown bread without a mixer. I can mix and knead, fold and press, lift and turn, sprinkle with flour and wipe away, intuit that the dough needs to be worked harder to loosen the gluten so it becomes soft and elastic. If it gets too hard, I throw it down on the surface from a height a few times and then it softens and gets sticky again.

I learned how to do all this and, through practice, it has become second nature. It's all cultural heritage. Cultural heritage in my hands. Methods developed over generations that are far from out of date.

The self-reliant community

I insist on picking my own chanterelles, carefully removing the fresh dirt from each one as I work my way through a dauntingly big pile. I also insist on making my own *pinnekjøtt* – the dried, salted rack of lamb that Norwegians traditionally eat at Christmas; and I have to say, it tastes very different from what you buy in the shops. I don't save any money by doing it – you can buy *pinnekjøtt* for about the same price that I pay to buy my lamb straight from the farmer – and if I were to factor in the time I spent gathering the chanterelles in the forest, they would quickly become very expensive. But that's not why I do it. My mushrooms and *pinnekjøtt* have a value that's far greater than money, greater even than taste – they have the value of being something that is 100 per cent pure and mine from scratch.

Is it irrational to derive pleasure from the extra time it takes, when you could get the same thing faster and cheaper elsewhere? Isn't it just an added expense and an unnecessary complication that has no place in a rational society? We humans have too many emotions for rationality at times.

And that's never going to change. So perhaps we could make life easier for ourselves if we simply embraced this and deepened our understanding of our surroundings.

The picture-postcard town of Røros, a historic mining town now listed on the UNESCO World Heritage list, is a splendid of example how this tendency can be turned into an opportunity rather than a problem. With its traditional wooden buildings and festive markets, Røros appears to be swathed in the national romanticism of bygone years – can they teach us anything about what is genuine, forward-looking and even profitable?

In order to test if there really is any contradiction between romantic and authentic, outdated and profitable, I plan my trip to Røros for the weekend of the Christmas market, when it's at its picture-postcard best. A perfect amount of snow lies on the jumble of small, colourful houses on the main street.

Your eyes can feast on lights and candles, wheat-sheafs and coffee pots on the fire; your nose is treated to mulled wine, caramelised almonds and horse dung, your ears to sleigh bells and

171

church bells. Your toes long for traditional Røros felted boots, your fingers yearn for the fur coats worn by the horse-sleigh drivers. The queues for the 'Christmas ride' are long. Tourists snuggle down under the sheepskins in sledges decorated with torches and bells. The drivers are not allowed to wear Gore-Tex or any other modern winter clothes, only wool, leather and fur.

I'm the sort of person who would gag if this was a film set. Feel the kind of cloying sickness you get when you google the Santa Claus Village in Rovaniemi.

But Røros isn't like that. Even though most locals don't travel to work every day by horse and sleigh, horses were still used for farming here much later than anywhere else in the country. While the mines used the latest technology, there wasn't room for tractors in the small fields between the houses. And so the horse was king, and has now seamlessly made the transition into a new role as welcoming host. And that is why it's not nause-ating, but instead sends tingles down your spine.

Before I carry on, I should confess (if you haven't already guessed) that I'm fonder of Røros than most. What impresses me is the way in which the old and the new work side by side. The World Heritage Site is not only about preservation, it is also home to a number of modern developments, so you find traditional crafts alongside industrial robots and a pilot project for mass-customisation, farming alongside nomadic reindeer herding and the opportunity for outdoor activities in the surrounding national park. Røros is a rural community where they've understood that you have to build on what you've got – and they do it so well. There's always something going on. Despite having no more than 5,600 inhabitants, the town has two local papers, a local radio station and a television station.

'And we need it – there's so much happening here,' I was once told by a woman who had invited me here to give a talk.

'It's such a traditional town, yet it's so alive,' says Lexie, a potter who came here from Scotland to work in Potteriet, the local pottery.

In the midst of the Christmas-market chaos, I have succeeded in arranging a meeting with the manager of Potteriet. The pottery is based in a building that was once a wool factory. Like most things in Røros, the pottery is not a particularly old business (after all, the town dates back no more than 300 years). It was started in 1993, as an initiative to combat unemployment. But, as with so much in Røros, it is firmly rooted in tradition.

The idea was that Potteriet would work with traditional ceramics from Trøndelag. Not because Røros was famous for its pottery, but because it has always been a bastion of craft.

Potteriet's manager, Robin Schellenberg, loves this craft environment. He claims to be part-Røros, part-Swiss. His father is a surgeon and his brother is a lumberjack, who works in 'the old-fashioned way', which in Switzerland means with horses or a funicular railway. It can be tricky work: after a storm, the trees often lie scattered like pick-up-sticks on the steep mountainsides, and you need to know what you are doing before you do anything at all.

'I always appreciated the beauty and dignity of manual work, but started out by studying languages. I enjoyed it, but I missed working with my hands.'

Then he came across the address of a glass-blowing school in Sweden. He spent three years there, practising industrial glass-blowing, before going to Denmark to learn glass design. And from there, he came to Røros.

'I'm happy here. There are so many riches to be found in Røros. The town's history is both valued and alive. Over time, people have learned to see the benefit of being a World Heritage Site and to look after what is old,' Robin says. This includes handicrafts and food production, as well as folk music and dance and *bunad* traditions. But this appreciation of their World Heritage status was not automatic. The copper mines in Røros closed for good in 1977. Three years later, the inhabitants were told by the authorities that not only were they not allowed to carry on as before, they were not even allowed to manage the transition themselves, but instead had to comply with rigid conservation regulations. This was not well received.

However, a little more than four decades later, all this has changed. There is remarkably little discussion about conservation in Røros these days. Traditional food, old houses and museums exist side by side with one of the largest office chair manufacturers in Europe and a SINTEF centre for applied research, technology and innovation, where the rest of the country can learn about mass-customisation.

And while the rest of the country has seen Norwegian wool as little more than a waste product to be dumped on the world market, Rørøs Tweed now produces throws and blankets that have acquired almost cult status, and sell for ten times as much as a throw from IKEA. The same is true of the cups from Potteriet, for which people happily pay perhaps 100 times more.

In Norway, Røros – the name and the brand – has become synonymous with quality and tradition. Rørosmeieriet, an organic dairy company, has made a commercial success of fermented milk, using a culture that uses leaves from the common butterwort.

The town may not have a long history, but it is an extremely rich vein, if you dig deep enough, and the people here have it in their blood.

You're allowed to have roots in Røros. Allowed to be proud of where you come from. At the same time, the people there are not afraid of using these roots to branch out into something new. More than a quarter of those employed in the municipality work in the manufacturing industry, which is more than three times the national average.[25]

Is there a connection between how we value manual and practical work and the process of centralisation which has seen the depopulation of rural communities?

The population of Røros is growing. Today, in 2020, there are 5,572 people living in the municipality. The government statistics bureau, Statistics Norway, has predicted that this will have increased to 6,201 by 2040.

Not all local authorities can support a university, a district court, a private research centre, municipal administration or other employment opportunities for people with higher education, of course. But they can all have small businesses. They could all have a manufacturing industry, on a scale to suit the local population. Not least the primary industries: forestry, agriculture and fishing – industries that need manual labour.

I come away from my visit to Røros thinking about the patterns of migration across the country and the shifting nature of the economy. And I wonder if it might all come back to the way we view our working hands.

SIX

In which I sit and watch the birds

My privy at the cabin is almost finished. The four corner posts stand firmly in the ground, the door and window are in place, the shingles are securely on the wall, the rainwater runs off the covering that I've laid on the roof, just as it should, and the first branches in the juniper wattle have turned orange – just as they should too.

Am I entitled to boast that I've created the closeness I hoped for, shortened the distance between material and product? The juniper wattle and shingles have become routine work, no longer as exciting, but they're still gratifying to do and there is always room for improvement.

Gathering building materials from around the cabin not only brings variation to otherwise monotonous work, it also gives the structure a kind of harmony. The first juniper-clad wall doesn't look so strange when it's joined by two other equally green, bushy and prickly friends.

As winter deepens, the challenges change. The days are shorter, so there's less light to work by, and it takes more time and effort to keep the cabin warm and put food on the table.

The old timber walls take a while to heat up. Generally, I choose to do the two-hour drive and thirty-minute walk in the evening, so I'm ready to start work as soon as it's light the next day. The first thing I have to do when I get there is fire up the black wood-burner in the kitchen. The draw in the chimney is not the best, and when the temperature drops below zero outside, it can sometimes be difficult to get it to light properly – and cold fingers don't make it any easier.

I soon start to understand what people mean when they say you need to know your burner. I realise that I don't need to be so wary of the half-burned logs that are left there from before, that I shouldn't stuff the burner full of newspaper, but should rather take the time to split the remaining wood into as small pieces as possible, and that the wax that is always left at the bottom of tea lights is worth its weight in gold.

After about an hour, when the draw is good and the chimney pipe is starting to warm, I can light the burner in the living room as well. It doesn't help to heat the walls as much as the one in the kitchen, but it's cosy sitting in the armchair right by the fire. The cabin walls never get properly warm the first evening anyway. But the temperature starts to rise quickly the next morning, and by the end of work on day two, there's a chance you might even be able to take your hat off indoors after the fire has been burning for a few hours.

The burners are greedy. Spruce wood burns quickly. It's not long before I've gone through the three piles of branches I'd amassed while I was clearing the trees. Fortunately, I can now turn a tree into firewood in a single day: I can fell it, strip it, chop it, split it and stack it.

The work is satisfying, because it's varied. There is excitement in the felling, whereas cutting all the twigs and branches off is boring; chopping is hard and laborious work, especially in snow, but using a chainsaw is fun. Even after reading Lars Mytting's *Norwegian Wood: Chopping, Stacking, and Drying Wood the Scandinavian Way*, I take no delight

185

whatsoever in the detail of stacking. My moment is splitting the wood.

To be honest, I never dreamed I would ever become so well acquainted with the axe. I had barely held an axe before I was twenty-five, so it's really no surprise that I was clumsy to begin with. But it doesn't help to be reminded of that fact when you fail to hit the large, round logs time and again, while the others around you split them into small sticks without any problem. It's often hard for me to be humble and open enough to learn from someone who knows more. But I'm working on it.

Meanwhile, I'm proud to say that I have become friends with the axe through trial and error, all on my own. Where no one can see me. I have discovered there's no secret to splitting wood, it just takes practice, practice and practice. With every chop, my body learns what it has to do, the movement settles in my muscles until I manage to get it right most of the time.

This whole building project has given me the opportunity to try things out, to play and to make mistakes, to discover a new side of myself. It has been heavy work and frustrating at times, but more importantly, it has also given me a peace that I seldom feel. And it has satisfied my need to create: to use my hands physically and practically.

My objective was to achieve something. Not to cobble something together, take it apart and then put it back together again until it was perfect, but to achieve a result. You don't need to be super handy to try to create something.

As has always been and always will be the case, not everything needs to be perfect; if it did, no one would ever get going with anything. You just have to make a start, to feel the excitement of building something, even if it is a slightly wonky but utterly charming privy. The whole point is the feeling you get when you imagine how you want it to be, and know what steps you need to take to get there, which tools you need, right down to finer details like whether the roofing screws have hex heads or not, because then you'll need a hex adaptor for the drill. I know, because I have learned through experience.

The privy at the cabin has given me new hands. I love my hands after a day's work on a wall, or the roof or floor. My wrists even feel like they've got wider, though I know it's just my imagination. But I'm in no doubt that my hands get wiser the more hard skin I have on my fingers.

This whole book can be summed up by the motto 'conservation through use'. From nimble fingers to the wider landscape, nothing should be left unused. Nothing is worth the paper it's printed on if the words are not followed up with action.

So now, let's get up and out. Get out and build. Get out and work, dig, hammer, whittle, chop, screw, fell, plant, gather, weed, slaughter. Let's get up and spin, sew, fix, break, measure, create, bake, rake, steam, iron, toil, labour and play.

And then suddenly, one evening, my privy is finished. The next morning, I sit there. I leave the door open. Through the gap, I can just see a corner of the cabin. And I'll be damned if a little goldcrest doesn't land on one of the spruce trees out there.

I sit for a long time, but I'm not going to tell you what it felt like to be inside a building I'd made from scratch, by hand. I think you can imagine for yourself. So instead, I'll just say: I don't think it will be the last thing I build.

AFTERWORD

*In which I get a new playground
and put down roots*

The privy, and the cabin to which it is attached, have shown me roots I didn't know I had. The cabin is the only place that is a constant in my life, and recently I've been there more than ever, and I want to carry on being there.

But, in an unexpected way, this story also ends up being about a different journey home.

Just a short time after finishing the privy, an email drops into my inbox to say that my partner and I have successfully bought a house. The first house I've ever owned. And it's not just any house: it's a house that I visited frequently as a child, because it's in the village where I grew up. In Holmedal. So that's where I'm now living.

If I look up from my desk, I can see the fjord I grew up with, the school I was frustrated with, the church I was not confirmed in – and the factory that I love so much. If I open the bedroom window and have a lie-in one morning, I'll hear the drop-hammer working. I can cycle down to see my little brother and have a cup of instant coffee in the office (although, actually, he's invested in a coffee machine now, of which I heartily approve). And best of all, I can be at the cabin within little more than half an hour.

Why move here? The house is quite old, but not dilapidated; cosy, but not too small. It's a red building, complete with a beautiful, special tree: in Scandinavia we call it a *tuntre* – a tree planted simply to stand by the house and grow and make us feel at home. We have berry bushes and big paving stones in the yard that faces a *stabbur* – an old storehouse from the 1800s, with a gallery and big stone fireplace. At the back of the house, there's a building big enough for a workshop; we can have a saw in there, and perhaps some meat-processing equipment. Maybe I can even make cheese and tan leather, and if we ever get a four-oared *færing* boat, it can be hoisted up and stored under the ceiling of the garage in winter. We don't have any fields or barns, but there is more than enough room for hens and rabbits.

In fact, the outdoor space and outbuildings are

more important to me than the house itself. There is plenty of good old-fashioned space, which feels new and exciting to me. Space to create. Room to play. Room to build. Room to potter – to do something at your own speed, to do something you want to do. Because you enjoy it. That's what is important.

There is, of course, room to potter everywhere and I could have found it elsewhere, but this particular house is here. The idea of moving home did not involve any romantic notions of returning to the innocence of childhood. Dalsfjord is beautiful, but so are many other fjords. I enjoyed living where we did before, out by the sea. Two hours' drive had been just the right distance from home. Until now. Because now I have something else to offer: my hands.

My bare hands have brought me home.

NOTES

1   Statistics Norway: Table 09174: *Lønn sysselsetting og produktivitet, etter næring*, sourced 1 October 2018.

2   Ibid.

3   O. K. Årdal, J. E. A. Chavez and S. Vepsä: 'Vi må snakke om sløyd', nrk.no, 22 September 2019.

4   Ronny Spaans: 'Kunsten å utmatte elevar', *Dag og Tid*, 9 February 2018.

5   Merlin Donald: *Origins of the Modern Mind*, Harvard University Press, 1993.

6   *Generell del av læreplane: Det skapende mennesket* https://www.udir.no/globalassets/upload/larerplaner/ generell_del/generell_del_lareplanen_bm.pdf

7   *Kjerneelementer og begrunnelser for valg av innhold i faget: Kunst og håndvert og duodji*, https://hoering.udir.no/ LastNedVedlegg/506

8   A. Gustavsen and H. Gjertsen: *'Det er de små skrittene som teller. Økt kunnskap om praksisnær opplæring i grunnleggende ferdigheter i kriminalomsorgen*, Nordland Research Institute, 10 February 2015. http://www.kriminalomsorgen.no/getfile.php/ 2998184.823.abwydytacs/Rapport+Praksisn%C3%A6r +oppl%C3%A6ring.pdf

9   Historian Fredrik W. Thue to Siri Helle: 'Utdanna til
    uvisse', *Dag og Tid*, 4 April 2014.

10 Jo Røed Skårderud: 'Henter fram verktøyene',
    Klassekampen, 22 December 2016.

11 Margunn Ueland: 'Hvorfor gjør de ikke som Vigrestad
    storskule?', *Stavanger Aftenblad*, 22 September 2017.

12 K. Furu, V. Hjellevik, I. Hartz, Ø. Karlstad, S. Skurtveit,
    H. S. Blix, H. Strøm and R. Selmer: *Legemiddelbruk hos
    barn og unge i Norge 2008–2017*, Folkehelseinstituttet,
    2018.

13 A. Reneflot, L. E. Aarø, H. Aase, T. Reichborn-
    Kjennerud, K. Tambs and S. Øverland: *Psykisk helse i
    Norge*, Folkehelseinstituttet, 2018. Susanne Dietrichson:
    'Kroppspress, skole og bekymringer gjør flere jenter
    psykisk syke', kjønnsforskning.no, 15 February 2018.

14 H. Kringstad: 'Halve befolkningen går under 500 meter
    per dag', *Adresseavisen*, 25 May 2015.

15 'Physical activity is an overarching concept, which
    includes many other terms related to physical
    movement including sport, exercise, training, outdoor
    life, play, work, personal fitness, physical education,
    etc.' Quote from the Norwegian Directorate of
    Health's definition of physical activity, *Statistikk om
    fysisk aktivitetsnivå og stillesitting* https://www.
    helsedirektoratet.no/%20tema/fysisk-aktivitet/
    statistikk-om-fysisk-aktivitetsniva-og-stillesitting

16 *Fysisk aktivitet for barn, unge, voksne, eldre og gravide*
    https://www.helsedirektoratet.no/faglige-rad/fysisk-
    aktivitet-for-barn-unge-voksne-eldre-og-gravide/
    stillesitting-begrense-tiden-i-ro#tiden-i-ro-bor-begrenses-
    og-stykkes-opp-med-mer-aktive-perioder

17   Stein Knardahl: 'Hvorfor er tungt arbeid skadelig hvis
     trening er sunt?' https://stami.no/hvorfor-er-tungt-
     arbeid-skadelig-hvis-trening-er-sunt/

18   Anders Ohnstad: *Gardssoga for Aurland I, Vassbygdi og
     fjellgardane*, Aurland Sogelag, 1988.

19   Statistics Norway: Table 04607: *Areal av korn og
     oljevekster*, by region, statistical variable and year.

20   Statistics Norway: https://www.ssb.no/arbeid-og-lonn/
     lonn-og-arbeidskraftkostnader/statistikk/lonn

21   Anders Bryn, Bjørn Egil Flø, Karoline Daugstad, Petter
     Dybedal and Heidi Vinge: *Cultour: Cultural landscapes of
     tourism and hospitality*, end report and conference report
     from the NFR project, 2013.

22   UNESCO: 'Convention for the Safeguarding of the
     Intangible Cultural Heritage', Paris, 17 October 2003.

23   The five organisations are: Norsk senter for folkemusikk
     og folkedans (Norwegian Centre for Folk Music and
     Dance), Norsk håndverksinstitutt (Norwegian Crafts
     Institute), Norges Husflidslag (Norwegian Folk Art and
     Craft Association), Forbundet KYSTEN (Norwegian
     Coastal Federation) and Norsk etnologisk gransking
     (Norwegian Ethnological Research) at the Norwegian
     Folk Museum. Bygdekvinnelaget (Rural Women's
     Association) has since been appointed as well.

24   Unfortunately I have managed to lose my notes on which
     blog this comes from. Apologies.

25   Statistics Norway: Registered employment, 27 per cent in
     Røros compared with 8 per cent in the rest of the country.
     https://www.ssb.no/kommunefakta/roros